KU-618-775

The **AA POCKET**Guide
VENICE

Venice: Regions and Best places to see

Original text by Teresa Fisher. Updated by Tim Jepson

© Automobile Association Developments Limited 2008. First published 2008

ISBN: 978-0-7495-5767-6

Published by AA Publishing, a trading name of Automobile Association Developments Limited, whose registered office is Fanum House, Basing View, Basingstoke, Hampshire RG21 4EA. Registered number 1878835.

Automobile Association Developments Limited retains the copyright in the original edition © 1991 and in all subsequent editions, reprints and amendments

Colour separation: Keenes, Andover
Printed and bound in Italy by Printer Trento S.r.l.

Front cover images: (t) AA/C Sawyer; (b) AA/A Mockford & N Bonetti
Back cover image: AA/D Miterdiri

A03604
Maps in this title produced from:
map data © New Holland Publishing (South Africa) (PTY) Limited 2007
mapping © ISTITUTO GEOGRAFICO DE AGOSTINI S.p.A., NOVARA 2007
Transport map © Communicarta Ltd, UK

About this book

Symbols are used to denote the following categories:

➕ map reference
✉ address or location
☎ telephone number
🕓 opening times
✋ admission charge
🍴 restaurant or café on premises
　 or nearby
Ⓜ nearest underground train station

🚌 nearest bus/tram route
🚆 nearest overground train station
⛴ nearest ferry stop
✈ nearest airport
❓ other practical information
ℹ tourist information office
➤ indicates the page where you will
　 find a fuller description

This book is divided into five sections.

Planning pages 14–27
Before you go; Getting there; Getting around; Being there

Best places to see pages 28–49
The unmissable highlights of any visit to Venice

Exploring pages 50–117
The best places to visit in Venice, organized by area

Excursions pages 118–129
Places to visit out of town

Maps pages 133–144
All map references are to the atlas section. For example, Palazzo Ducale has the reference ➕ 139 C8 – indicating the grid square in which it can be found

Contents

Planning

Before you go

WHEN TO GO

JAN	FEB	MAR	APR	MAY	JUN	JUL	AUG	SEP	OCT	NOV	DEC
6°C	8°C	12°C	15°C	20°C	23°C	26°C	25°C	21°C	16°C	12°C	7°C
43°F	46°F	54°F	59°F	68°F	73°F	79°F	77°F	70°F	61°F	54°F	45°F

High season   Low season

The best times to visit Venice are March to early June and mid-September to the end of October, when the weather is generally fine but not too hot. Avoid July and August, when the city is not only hot but also often extremely crowded. Winters can be very cold and damp, with chill easterly winds and mists off the lagoon. Snow is uncommon, but always possible. However, bear in mind that this is a city that is beautiful, and has plenty to offer, whatever the weather, but can be busy year-round. Particularly crowded times are during Carnevale (usually around 10 days in February), Easter, Christmas, New Year and during school holidays.

WHAT YOU NEED

● Required
○ Suggested
▲ Not required

Some countries require a passport to remain valid for a minimum period (usually at least six months) beyond the date of entry – check before you travel.

	UK	Germany	USA	Netherlands	Spain
Passport (or National Identity Card where applicable)	●	●	●	●	●
Visa (regulations can change – check before you travel)	▲	▲	▲	▲	▲
Onward or Return Ticket	▲	▲	▲	▲	▲
Health Inoculations (tetanus and polio)	▲	▲	▲	▲	▲
Health Documentation (► 17, Health Insurance)	●	●	●	●	●
Travel Insurance	○	○	○	○	○
Driving Licence (national)	●	●	●	●	●
Car Insurance Certificate	●	●	●	●	●
Car Registration Document	●	●	●	●	●

WEBSITES

Tourist Authority
www.turismovenezia.it

City Council
www.comune.venezia.it

Italian State Tourist Office
www.enit.it

Venice Transport Authority
www.actv.it

TOURIST OFFICES AT HOME

In the UK
Italian State Tourist Office (ENIT)
1 Princes Street
London W1B 2AY
☎ 020 7493 6695
www.enit.it;
www.italiantourism.com

In the US
Italian State Tourist Office (ENIT)
630 Fifth Avenue
Suite 1565
Rockefeller Center
New York, NY 10111
☎ 212/245-4822 or 212/245-5618

HEALTH INSURANCE

Nationals of EU and certain other countries can get reduced-cost emergency healthcare in Italy with the relevant documentation – an EHIC (European Health Insurance Card), although private medical insurance is still advised and is essential for all other visitors.

Dental treatment is expensive in Italy but should be covered by private medical insurance. A list of dentists *(dentisti)* can be found in the yellow pages of the telephone directory or online at www.paginegialle.it

TIME DIFFERENCES

| GMT | Venice | Germany | USA (NY) | Netherlands | Spain |
| 12 noon | 1PM | 1PM | 7AM | 1PM | 1PM |

Venice is one hour ahead of Greenwich Mean Time (GMT +1), but from late March, when clocks are put forward one hour, until late October, Italian summer time (GMT +2) operates.

NATIONAL HOLIDAYS

1 Jan *New Year's Day*
6 Jan *Epiphany*
Mar/Apr *Easter Monday*
25 Apr *Liberation Day and patron saint's day (San Marco)*

1 May *Labour Day*
15 Aug *Assumption of the Virgin*
1 Nov *All Saints' Day*
8 Dec *Feast of the Immaculate Conception*

Conception
25 Dec *Christmas Day*
26 Dec *Santo Stefano*

WHAT'S ON WHEN

January *Regata della Befana* (6 Jan): The first of more than 100 regattas to be held on the lagoon throughout the year is on Epiphany.

February *Carnevale* (10 days before Lent): The carnival was abolished by the French in 1797 but revived in 1979 with great success. At first largely a Venetian festival, it is now international and, some complain, over-elaborate. Masks and fancy dress – which can be bought or rented in the city – are worn all day and most of the night. A daily schedule of events includes dancing at night in a *campo*, where mulled wine and traditional sugared cakes are sold from stands.

April *Festa di San Marco* (25 Apr): The feast day of St Mark, Venice's patron saint. A gondola race from Sant'Elena to the Punta della Dogana marks the day and men give women a red rose.

May *Festa della Sensa* (Sunday after Ascencion Day): the Mayor of Venice re-enacts the ceremony of the Marriage of Venice with the Sea. In the old days, the Doge would be rowed out to sea in his ceremonial barge to cast a gold wedding ring into the Adriatic, but the occasion is now only a faint echo of the original.
Vogalonga (Sunday following *La Sensa*): a 32km (20-mile) rowing race in which anyone can join in any type of oared boat from San Marco to Burano and back.

June *Biennale* (every odd-numbered year Jun–end Sep): International arts exhibition.
Festa di San Pietro (last weekend in Jun): Celebrates the feast of St Peter; centred on his church in Castello, it's a lively event with concerts, dancing and food stands.

July *Festa del Redentore* (third weekend in Jul): Involves the building of a bridge of boats across the Giudecca Canal to the church of the Redentore and was begun as a festival in thanksgiving for the ending of a plague more than four centuries ago. Picnics and fireworks.

August/September *Mostra del Cinema Venezia* (12 days from last week in Aug): The high-profile international Venice Film Festival is held on the Lido; it's Italy's version of Cannes.

September *Regata Storica* (first Sunday in Sep): The most spectacular event of the Venetian year, it involves gondola races and a procession up the Grand Canal of boats and barges manned by Venetians in historic costume.

November *Festa della Salute* (21 Nov): A procession makes its way across the Grand Canal on floating bridges to the church of the Salute to give thanks for the ending of another plague of 1630.

December *La Befana* (Christmas, New Year): Celebrations for the festive season.

Getting there

BY AIR

Marco Polo Airport		
🚤	50 minutes	
🚌	25 minutes	
🚗	15 minutes	
13km (8 miles) to city centre		

Treviso Airport		
🚤	N/A	
🚌	45 minutes	
🚗	35 minutes	
30km (19 miles) to city centre		

There are direct flights to Venice from all over the world. Scheduled flights arrive at Venice's Marco Polo airport, while the city's second airport, Treviso, caters mostly for charter and no-frills airlines.

BY RAIL

International and national rail services arrive at Venice's main railway station, Venezia Santa Lucia (Venezia SL), at the western end of the Grand Canal. Boats to most parts of the city leave from outside the station. Some rail services stop at Venezia Mestre, on the mainland, and do not cross the causeway to Venice.

BY CAR

The A4 *autostrada* (motorway) runs close to Mestre for the most direct approach to Venice by car. However, it is not recommended to bring cars to Venice itself. Queues to cross the causeway to the city can be long and all cars must be left in expensive multi-storey car parks at Piazzale Roma. There are no exceptions: illegally parked cars will be towed. It is better to find secure parking in Mestre and take the train or dispense with a car.

BY SEA

Ferries run to Venice from ports across the Adriatic in Croatia, Slovenia and elsewhere. Many cruise liners also dock in the city.

Getting around

PUBLIC TRANSPORT

Vaporetto The *vaporetto*, or water bus, is operated by the public transport system, ACTV; www.actv.it. The main routes run every 10 to 20 minutes during the day. Services are reduced in the evening, especially after midnight. A night service (N) runs along the Grand Canal. You can buy a ticket for each journey (€5 or €2 for one stop on the Grand Canal) at a ticket office on the pier (if there is one) or pay more for a ticket on board, but if you intend to make several journeys in a day, buy a *biglietto giornaliero* (24-hour ticket; €12). If you plan to use the boats a lot over three days, buy a *biglietto ore* (72-hour; €25). All tickets must be date-stamped by the automatic machine on the pier before boarding. If you are staying a week, you can buy a weekly *abbonamento* from ticket offices.

Gondola A gondola is undoubtedly the most enjoyable means of transport in the city, but also the most expensive – around €80 for four passengers. Fares are governed by a tariff for a 50-minute trip, with a surcharge for night trips after 8pm, but, as gondoliers are notorious for overcharging, it is often easiest to establish terms by ordering a gondola via your tour representative or hotel staff. For a memorable outing, take a two-hour gondola ride down the Grand Canal with a picnic supper on board (note that the side canals are usually much calmer). Or take a cruise operated during the summer months by flotillas of gondolas packed with tourists and entertained by singers – providing an ideal opportunity to explore the waterways at an affordable price.

Traghetto Ferry gondolas – *traghetti* – cross the Grand Canal between special piers at seven different points, providing a vital service for pedestrians. They are indicated by a yellow street sign, illustrated with a tiny gondola symbol. The very reasonable fare (as little as €0.50) is paid to the gondolier when you board.

WATER TAXI

Water-taxis can be rented from water taxi stands, including ones at the airport and Piazza San Marco. They can also be ordered by telephone (☎ 041 522 2303; www.motoscafivenezia.it). Fares are very expensive, but are regulated by a tariff.

DRIVING

- Italians drive on the right.
- Seat belts must be worn in front seats at all times and in rear seats where fitted.

- Random breath-testing takes place. Never drive under the influence of alcohol.
- Fuel *(benzina)* is more expensive than in the US and most European countries. Filling stations all sell unleaded fuel *(senza piombo)*, but do not always accept credit cards. They are generally open Monday to Saturday 7–12:30, 3–7:30. Motorway service stations open 24 hours.
- In the event of a breakdown call the Automobile Club d'Italia (☎ 116), giving your location, registration number and type of car, and the nearest ACI office will tow you to the nearest ACI garage. This service is free to foreign vehicles, but you will need to produce your car documentation and passport.
- Speed limits are as follows:
  On motorways *(autostrade)* 130kph (80mph)
  On main roads: 110kph (68mph)
  On secondary roads: 90kph (56mph)
  In towns: 50kph (31mph)

CAR RENTAL

The leading international car rental companies have offices at Marco Polo airport. Book a car in advance (essential in peak season) either direct or through a travel agent. Bear in mind that driving in the centre of Venice itself is not possible.

FARES AND CONCESSIONS

Students Holders of an International Student Identity Card may obtain some concessions on travel, entrance fees and so on. A 'Junior Venice Card' for those aged 14–29, available from tourist offices, offers discounts to museums, churches and on most ACTV bus and boat services. A second card, the Senior Venice Card, is available for those 30 and over. Both have 3- or 7-day options. The main youth hostel in Venice is Ostello Venezia, Fondamenta della Zitelle, on Giudecca (☎ 041 523 8211). Reserve well in advance.

Senior citizens Venice is a popular destination for older travellers although, due to the limited transport system, you must be prepared for lots of walking. The best deals are available through tour operators who specialize in tours for senior citizens. There are reductions for entry to museums for EU citizens over 60 years of age.

Being there

TOURIST OFFICES
Head Office
Palazzetto del Selva
Giardinetti Reale
San Marco
☎ 041 529 8711;
www.turismovenezia.it

Branches
International Arrivals Hall (airport office)
Marco Polo airport
☎ 041 541 5887

Ferrovia Santa Lucia (train station office)
☎ 041 529 8711
Piazza San Marco 71
☎ 041 529 8711

Piazzale Roma
☎ 041 529 8711

Gran Viale Santa Maria Elisabetta 6 (Lido office)
☎ 041 541 5721

MONEY
The euro (€) is the official currency of Italy. Banknotes are issued in denominations of 5, 10, 20, 50, 100, 200 and 500 euros; coins in denominations of 1, 2, 5, 10, 20 and 50 cents, and 1 and 2 euros.

TIPS/GRATUITIES

Yes ✓ No ✗		
Restaurants (if service not included)	✓	10–15%
Cafés/bars (if service not included)	✓	€1 minimum
Tour guides	✓	€1 minimum
Water-taxis	✓	10%
Chambermaids	✓	€2
Porters	✓	€1
Toilet attendants	✓	50c minimum

POSTAL SERVICES
Most post offices open Mon–Fri from 8–2. Some also open on Saturday morning. The main post office (ufficio postale) at Palazzo delle Poste (near the Rialto Bridge) is open Mon–Sat 8:30–6:30 (www.poste.it). You can also buy stamps (francobolli) at tobacconists (tabacchi), idenitified with a large 'T' sign.

TELEPHONES

Public telephones take coins, tokens *(gettone)* or phone cards *(schede telfoniche)* which can be bought from Telecom Italia (TI) offices (the state telephone company) or *tabacchi*, bars and newsstands. You have to break off the marked corner of the phonecard before use.

International dialling codes
From Venice to:
UK: 00 44
Germany: 00 49
Netherlands: 00 31
Spain: 00 34
USA: 00 1

Emergency telephone numbers
National Police (Polizia di Stato): 113
City Police (Carabinieri): 112
Fire (Vigili del Fuoco): 115
Ambulance (Ambulanza): 118

EMBASSIES AND CONSULATES

UK: ☎ 041 522 7207
USA in Milan: ☎ 02 290351
Germany: ☎ 041 523 7675

Netherlands: ☎ 041 528 3416
Spain: ☎ 041 523 3254

HEALTH ADVICE

Sun advice The sunniest (and hottest) months are June, July and August. You are advised to use a strong sunblock and avoid the midday sun.

Drugs Prescription and non-prescription drugs and medicines are available from a pharmacy *(farmacia)*, distinguished by a green cross.

Safe water Tap water is generally safe to drink unless marked *acqua non potabile*. Drink plenty of water in hot weather.

PERSONAL SAFETY
To help prevent crime:
- Do not carry more cash around with you than you need
- Beware of pickpockets in markets, tourist sights or crowded places
- The main police station, at Via San Nicoladi 22, Marghera (☎ 041 271 5772, 041 271 5586) has a special department to deal with visitors' problems

ELECTRICITY
The power supply is 220 volts, but is suitable for 240-volt appliances. Sockets accept two-round-pin Continental-style plugs. US visitors should bring a voltage transformer.

OPENING HOURS

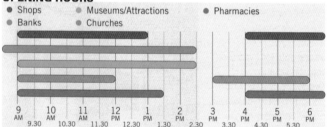

- Shops
- Banks
- Museums/Attractions
- Churches
- Pharmacies

| 9 AM | 10 AM | 11 AM | 12 PM | 1 PM | 2 PM | 3 PM | 4 PM | 5 PM | 6 PM |
| 9.30 | 10.30 | 11.30 | 12.30 | 1.30 | 2.30 | 3.30 | 4.30 | 5.30 | |

Many shops and supermarkets also open outside the times shown above, especially in summer. Most food shops close on Wednesday afternoons, while many other shops close Monday mornings (except in summer), and may close Saturday afternoon. Most shops are closed on Sundays. Some churches are permanently closed except during services; state-run museums usually close Mondays and some museums, such as the Correr, Palazzo Ducale and Guggenheim, stay open all day.

LANGUAGE

Many Venetians speak some English, but they really appreciate it when foreigners make an effort to speak Italian, however badly. It is relatively straightforward to have a go at some basics, as the words are pronounced as they are spelled. Every vowel and consonant (except 'h') is sounded and, as a general rule, the stress falls on the next-to-last syllable. Here is a basic vocabulary to help with the most essential words and expressions.

yes	*sì*	help!	*aiuto!*
no	*no*	today	*oggi*
please	*per favore*	tomorrow	*domani*
thank you	*grazie*	yesterday	*ieri*
hello	*ciao*	how much?	*quanto?*
goodbye	*arrivederci*	expensive	*caro*
goodnight	*buona notte*	open	*aperto*
sorry	*mi dispiace*	closed	*chiuso*
hotel	*albergo*	reservation	*prenotazione*
room	*camera*	rate	*tariffa*
..single/double	*..singola/doppia*	breakfast	*prima colazione*
..one/two nights	*per una/due notte/i*	toilet/bath/shower	*toilette/bagno/*
..one/two people	*..per una/due*		*doccia*
	persona/e	key	*chiave*
restaurant	*ristorante*	lunch	*pranzo/colazione*
café	*caffè*	dinner	*cena*
table	*tavolo*	starter	*il primo*
menu	*menù/carta*	main course	*il secondo*
set menu	*menù turistico*	dish of the day	*piatto del giorno*
wine list	*lista dei vini*	dessert	*dolci*
aeroplane	*aeroplano*	ferry	*traghetto*
airport	*aeroporto*	ticket	*biglietto*
train	*treno*	ticket office	*biglietteria*
bus	*autobus*	timetable	*orario*

Best places to see

1 Basilica di San Marco

This is one of the most visited places in Europe and should not be missed – the exotic Byzantine–Venetian basilica is simply one of the world's greatest medieval buildings.

The cathedral of Venice evokes the blending of East and West that is at the heart of the Venetian character. More Eastern than European, the architecture, the decoration and the atmosphere of ancient sanctity span both the centuries and styles of Mediterranean civilization.

Originally built to house the body of St Mark, the patron saint of Venice, which had been smuggled from its tomb in Alexandria by Venetian merchants in AD828, the basilica evolved its present appearance between the 9th and 19th centuries. The basic building dates from the late 11th century, the domes from the 13th and the decoration from subsequent centuries. Much of the decoration was plundered or presented to Venice during its time of supremacy, most notably the four famous gilded horses above the main doors. Probably made in the 4th century AD, they were looted from Constantinople, when it was sacked by the Venetians during the Crusades, and stood on the outside for nearly 600 years until plundered, in turn, by the French. After the Napoleonic wars, they were restored to the basilica although, due to atmospheric pollution, the originals are now kept in a gallery inside while replicas stand in their place.

Viewing the richness of ornament outside and

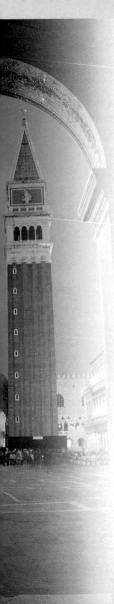

inside the basilica can occupy you for hours, but even the hurried visitor can admire the glowing gold of the mosaics that cover nearly half a hectare (1 acre) of the vaulting or examine them more closely from the galleries. If you don't have time to go inside, or the teeming crowds that engulf the Basilica prove too much for you, spend a few minutes taking in the exterior details. The central door's wonderful Romanesque carvings dating from the 13th century are considered the exterior's greatest treasures. Superbly carved, they show the earth, the seas and animals on the underside, with the virtues and the beatitudes on the outer face and the Zodiac and labours of the month on the inner.

If you have more time to go inside make sure you see the gold Byzantine altarpiece, the Pala d'Oro. Encrusted with over 2,600 pearls, rubies, emeralds and other precious stones, it was begun in the 10th century but not completed until 1342.

The Basilica has been the cathedral of Venice only since 1807. Before that time it had been the shrine of San Marco and the chapel of the Doge, while the church of San Pietro di Castello in the far east of the city (➤ 74) had been the cathedral, an arrangement to minimize the influence of the Papacy on the affairs of Venice.

🚻 139 C8 ⊠ Piazza San Marco 1 🕐 Oct–Apr Mon–Sat 9:45–5:30, Sun 2–4; Nov–Mar Mon–Sat 9:45–4:30, Sun 2–4 ✋ Basilica free. Museo Marciano, Treasury and Pala d'Oro inexpensive 🍴 Piazza San Marco (€€€) 🚤 Vallaresso/ San Zaccaria

2 Canal Grande

This must be one of the best places in the world to take a boat trip. Take in all the city's finest palaces and scenes of Venetian life along the way.

Following the course of an original creek through the muddy islands of the lagoon, the serpentine canal sweeps in two great curves from what is now the Santa Lucia rail station to the Basin of San Marco. It varies in width from 40–70m (130–230ft), has a maximum depth of 5.5m (18ft) and is crossed by three main bridges – the Scalzi, the Rialto and the Accademia – and seven *traghetto* (ferry gondola) routes.

Travelling eastwards along the Canal, some of the principal buildings between the station and the Rialto Bridge are, on the left, the Scalzi, San Geremia and San Marcuola and Ca' Labia (Tiepolo frescoes), Ca' Vendramin-Calergi (the Municipal Casino in winter) and the Ca' d'Oro (museum and art gallery). On the right are San Simeone Piccolo and San Stae, Fondaco dei Turchi (Natural History Museum), Ca' Pesaro (Museums of Modern Art and Oriental Art) and Ca' Favretto (Hotel San Cassiano) – and then the fish, fruit and vegetable markets just before the Rialto Bridge.

Between the Rialto and the Accademia bridges are, on the left, the church of San Samuele and the Ca' Mocenigo (not to be confused with the Palazzo Mocenigo, which is open to the public) and Palazzo Grassi; on the right, Ca' Rezzonico (museum of 18th-century arts) – then, at the Accademia Bridge, the Accademia Gallery in the former church and *scuola* (school) of Santa Maria della Carità. Between the Accademia Bridge and the Basin of San Marco are, on the left, Ca' Barbaro, Ca' Grande (Prefecture of Police), Ca' Gritti-Pisani (Gritti Palace Hotel), Ca' Tiepolo (Europa e Regina Hotel) and the buildings around Piazza San Marco.

On the right are the church of Santa Maria della Salute and the palaces of Ca' Venier dei Leoni (housing the Peggy Guggenheim Collection of Modern Art), Ca' Dario (its façade richly inlaid with multi-coloured marble) and, at the extreme end, the Dogana di Mare (the Customs House).

✚ 134 D1–140 D1 ✉ Piazza San Marco 🚤 1, 2 (plus 3, 4 in summer)

3 Gallerie dell'Accademia

www.gallerieaccademia.org

This is the intimate home to some of the best of Venetian art spanning the 14th to the 18th centuries, from Byzantine to baroque.

The most famous and comprehensive collection of Venetian painting is housed in this former church, monastery and scuola at the Dorsoduro side of the wooden Accademia Bridge (one of the three crossing points of the Canal Grande). Most paintings come from palaces and churches in the city, and although it would have been more appropriate to see them in their original settings, here they are grouped in galleries and are well lit.

Usually some galleries are closed for various reasons, but there is always enough on display to delight and even sometimes to cause visual and mental indigestion – try to avoid Sundays, which are particularly busy. Highlights include Giovanni Bellini's *Madonna Enthroned* and Carpaccio's *The Presentation of Jesus* in Room II; Giorgione's *Tempest* and Bellini's *Madonna of the Trees* in Room V; Titian's *St John the Baptist* in Room VI; three magnificent paintings by Veronese in Room XI; the Accademia's only Canaletto and six charming 18th-century *Scenes from Venetian Life* by Longhi in Room XVII; and Carpaccio's enchanting series of paintings illustrating *The Legend of St Ursula*, portraying the clothes and settings of 15th-century Venice, in Room XXI.

✠ 138 D4 ✉ Campo della Carità, Dorsoduro 1023 ☎ 041 522 2247 ⏰ Mon 8:15–2, Tue–Sun 8:15–7:15 (last entrance at 6:45) ✋ Expensive; a combined ticket for the Accademia, the Ca' d'Oro and Museo d'Arte Orientale is a good buy 🚤 Accademia

4 Palazzo Ducale

www.museiciviciveneziani.it

The palace, a vast, grandiose civic building, is the cream of Italy's Gothic constructions.

Venice was governed from the Doges' Palace for a thousand years, and it still dominates the city. The pink palace, with its white colonnades that can be seen across the water from the Basin of San Marco, looks much as it did when it replaced an earlier building in the 14th century, except that its pillars seem foreshortened because the level of the surrounding path has been raised. Here the elected doge of Venice held his court and presided over a system of councils, designed to prevent any one self-interested faction from seizing power. Once, when this failed, the over-ambitious Doge Marin Falier was convicted of treason and beheaded at the top of the new marble staircase in the palace courtyard and his portrait replaced by a black cloth.

Visitors to the palace can marvel at the richly decorated council chambers on the second floor,

their walls and ceilings painted by the leading Venetian painters, including Tintoretto, whose *Paradise* is one of the largest old master paintings in the world. It graces the wall of the Sala del Maggior Consiglio (Great Council Chamber), a vast hall designed to seat 1,700 citizens who had the right to vote in the council. Have a look at the Armoury, with some 2,000 weapons and suits of armour.

From the Palace itself, the Ponte dei Sospiri (Bridge of Sighs) crosses a canal to the prison and the notorious, waterlogged dungeons below water level known as *pozzi* (the wells). You can join guided tours through the palace and the prison and also special tours of the 'secret rooms' (in English, French and Italian). This includes the interrogation rooms and torture chamber of the State Inquisitors and the cells under the roof of the prison, from which Casanova made his dramatic escape in 1756, while serving a five-year sentence on charges involving blasphemy, magic and espionage.

The Doges' Palace is so rich in art and architectural splendours that a whole morning or afternoon could be devoted to it. When Venice is crowded, it is best to arrive early to enjoy an unhurried tour. If you visit in winter be sure to dress warmly as the Palazzo Ducale has no heating and is extremely cold.

➕ 139 C8 ✉ Piazzetta di San Marco ☎ 041 520 9070/041 271 5911 🕒 Apr–Oct daily 9–7; Nov–Mar daily 9–5 🎟 Museum Card (valid for Museo Civico Correr, Museo Archeologico Nazionale, Sala Monumentali della Biblioteca Marciana) expensive 🍴 Café (€–€€) 🚤 Vallaresso/ San Zaccaria

5 Piazza San Marco

Visitors flock here in their thousands and it can be rather daunting, but the scale and spectacle of this piazza is breathtaking.

The Piazza San Marco is the heart of Venice. When Napoleon conquered the Venetian Republic he called it 'the most elegant drawing-room in Europe', and so it still is. At the eastern end stands the Basilica di San Marco with its Byzantine domes; to one side its campanile, the Piazzetta outside the Doges' Palace and the Basin of San Marco; to the other the Clock Tower and the Piazzetta dei Leoncini, named after the red marble lions standing there. The north side of the Piazza is bounded by the Procuratie Vecchie, the former offices of the Republic's administration, with an arcade of shops below and the Caffè Quadri, once patronised by the Austrian occupiers of Venice. On the south side is the former administration building, the Procuratie Nuove, with another arcade of shops and the Caffè Florian, the favourite of Venetian patriots during the Austrian occupation, below. At the western end of the Piazza, the church of San Geminiano was demolished on Napoleon's orders, and a new arcade with a ballroom above was built (the entrance of the Correr Museum of Venetian history is now there, ➤ 56). The two granite columns near the water's edge in the Piazzetta were set up in the 12th

century; one is surmounted by a stone Lion of St Mark, the other by the figure of St Theodore, the first patron saint of the city, proudly wielding shield and spear.

🚩 139 C7 ✉ Piazza San Marco 🍴 Florian (€–€€€) and Quadri (€–€€€) 🚤 Vallaresso/San Marco

6 San Giorgio Maggiore

A tranquil haven from the bustle of San Marco, this magnificent Palladian church has tremendous views from the campanile.

The church stands on its island across the Basin of San Marco, giving Venice one of its most celebrated views. Designed by Andrea Palladio in the 16th century, it has all the majesty that the term 'Palladian' implies, and this is particularly apparent at night when the dazzling marble façade is floodlit. Originally founded in 790, the first church was destroyed by an earthquake in 1223 and not rebuilt until Palladio began work in 1559, the 1443 monastery next door taking precedence. The result was worth waiting for – one of the finest example's of Italian neoclassical architecture, complete with four-columned portico. Don't miss the choir stalls, which have some of the finest wood carving in Venice.

The interior is vast and austere, its white stone a magnificent setting for its works of art, including paintings by Tintoretto and a bronze altarpiece, *The Globe Surmounted by God the Father*, dating from the 16th century.

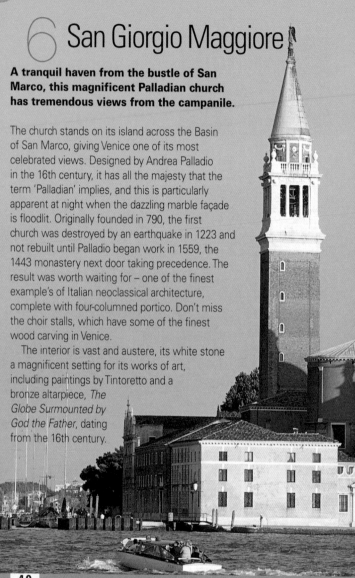

Other highlights by Tintoretto, splendidly offset by the light from the high windows, are *The Fall of Manna* and *The Last Supper* (both 1592–94), hung in the choir stalls. To the right of the choir stalls in the Cappela dei Morti is hung what may be Tintoretto's last work, *The Deposition* (1594).

The tall and slender campanile, ascended by an elevator, offers the best bird's-eye views of Venice. Unlike that of San Marco, it is detached from the city and can be seen as a panorama across the water.

141 E5 ✉ Campo San Giorgio, Isola San Giorgio Maggiore ☎ 041 522 7827 ⏱ May–Sep daily 9:30–12:30, 2:30–6:30; Oct–Apr daily 9:30–12:30, 2:30–4:30 ✋ Church free, campanile moderate 🚢 San Giorgio

7 Santi Giovanni e Paolo

Here is the resting place of more than 20 of the city's doges, buried beneath monumental tombs within a majestic Gothic church.

Called San Zanipolo by Venetians, the church stands to the north of San Marco. The largest church in Venice, it measures 101m (331ft) in length, is 38m (125ft) wide and 33m (108ft) high and was built by the Dominicans in the 14th and 15th centuries.

Despite its bulk, the red brick building is not ponderous, partly because of the cleaning of the elaborate Gothic portals at the west end and the monuments within. It is best seen on a sunny day as the interior can be dark on a dull day.

Inside, the original choir screen and stalls have not survived, leaving the nave light and airy. The church is commonly called the Pantheon of Doges, and around the walls stand magnificent monuments to doges and, among other notables, the Venetian general Marcantonio Bragadin, who was flayed alive by the Turks when they captured Cyprus in 1571. Not only does a fresco on the monument depict this, but the flayed skin, which was stolen from Constantinople, lies in a small sarcophagus. His death was avenged at the Battle of Lepanto by Doge Sebastiano Venier, whose fine bronze statue also stands in the church.

➕ 137 F5 ✉ Campo Santi Giovanni e Paolo, Castello 6363 ☎ 041 523 5913 🕐 Daily 7:30–12:30, 3:30–7:30. Closed during services 🚻 Free 🍴 Rosa Salva bar for coffee nearby (€) 🚤 Fondamenta Nove/Ospedale Civile

8 Santa Maria Gloriosa dei Frari

www.basilicadeifrari.it

Another superb Gothic building and Venice's second largest church, it is filled with magnificent paintings, monuments and ornate woodwork.

This church is Venice's second largest and has some impressive statistics. Built of brick, it is huge: 98m (322ft) long, 46m (151ft) wide and 28m (92ft) high, and dates from the 14th and 15th centuries. Reached through a maze of streets, it was the Franciscans' Venetian powerbase, originally founded in 1250. The church stands on the far side of the Canal Grande and is almost as large as Santi Giovanni e Paolo but has a wholly different character. The choir screen and stalls remain and the nave is shadowed

and sombre, as are the vast and elaborate monuments, including the open-doored vast white pyramid (1827) containing the heart of the 19th-century

sculptor Antonio Canova. He designed it as a monument to the great Venetian painter Titian (*d*1576), who, in fact, is buried across the aisle under a dramatic 19th-century statue.

Two paintings are the particular glories of the Frari. One is Titian's huge *The Assumption* (1516–18), still in the position for which it was painted above the high altar. The other is *The Madonna and Child* by Bellini in the sacristy, one of the loveliest paintings in Venice.

Like Santi Giovanni e Paolo (➤ 42–43), the Frari can easily occupy an hour or more for those with an interest in painting, sculpture and architecture.

🕂 138 A3 ✉ Campo dei Frari, San Polo ☎ 041 275 0462 or 041 275 0494 🕐 Mon–Sat 9–6, Sun 1–6 ✋ Inexpensive 🚊 San Tomà

9 Santa Maria della Salute

This great baroque church stands proudly at the entrance to the Grand Canal, one of the most imposing landmarks in the city.

Like the Redentore (▶ 103), this church was built to give thanks for the ending of a plague, but in the following century. The great domed church has sometimes been seen as the hostess of the city, welcoming visitors; as the novelist Henry James wrote: 'like some great lady on the threshold of her salon…with her domes and scrolls, her scalloped buttresses and statues forming a pompous crown,

and her wide steps disposed on the ground like the train of a robe'. After dark, a walk through the alleys of Dorsoduro can suddenly end on the brilliantly floodlit steps of the Salute beneath its gleaming bulk, the water below dancing with reflected light.

The magnificent baroque interior is more restrained and somewhat austere in comparision to the exuberant exterior. You can view an early Titian, *The Descent of the Holy Spirit* (1550), third on the left. Other fine paintings can be found in the sacristy, with eight more Titians, and Tintoretto's magnificent *Marriage Feast at*

Cana (1561). Look for his self-portrait – the artist is depicted as the first Apostle on the left. You have to pay an admission charge to see these paintings, but it's worth it.

Venetians come to the church on 21 November, the feast day of the Salute, to give thanks for good health.

✚ 139 D6 ✉ Campo della Salute, Dorsoduro, near the eastern end of the Grand Canal ☎ 041 522 5558
🕐 Apr–Sep daily 9–12, 3–6:30; Oct–Mar daily 9–12, 3–5:30. Sacristy Mon–Sat 10–11:30, 3–5, Sun 3–5
✋ Church free; sacristy inexpensive 🚤 Salute

10 Scuola Grande di San Rocco

www.scuolagrandesanrocco.it

Drawn in by the mastery of the cycle of 54 paintings by Tintoretto, you won't be disappointed by the stunning ornate interior.

This is the largest and grandest of the *scuole*, standing close to the church of the Frari. It was founded in honour of St Roch, who dedicated his life to the care of the sick. It is most celebrated for its great series of powerful paintings by Tintoretto depicting Biblical scenes, a monumental achievement covering the walls and ceilings of this magnificent *scuola*. It is best to start by heading up the great staircase to the Sala dell'Albergo, off the main hall, to see the works in the order Tintoretto painted them. The room is dominated by the powerful *Crucifixion* (1565), one of the greatest paintings in the world. In the main upper hall you will find striking ceiling

paintings depicting scenes from the Old Testament. The vast scenes on the walls depict episodes from the New Testament, showing his departure from contemporary ideas with wonderful use of colour, form and light.

Coming back downstairs to the Ground Floor Hall you will find the final paintings in Tintoretto's cycle, a culmination of 23 years of work. Here the artist is at his most sublime, as seen in the execution of the *Annunciation* and the *Flight into Egypt*. These reflect the artist's later style, and the use of dramatic light is revolutionary for its time. In addition to these superb paintings and ornate interior, look for the beautiful carvings below the paintings, works by 17th-century sculptor Francesco Pianta.

🔁 138 B3 ✉ Campo San Rocco, San Polo 3052 ☎ 041 523 4864 🕐 Apr–Oct daily 9–5:30; Nov–Mar daily 10–4 ✋ Moderate 🚤 San Tomà

SCVOLA GRANDE
DI SAN ROCCO
S|R

Exploring

Venice is divided into six *sestieri* (districts): to the north and east of the Grand Canal is San Marco in the centre, with Castello to the east; to the south and west lies Dorsoduro across the Grand Canal from San Marco with San Polo, then Santa Croce and finally Cannaregio to the north.

Each area has its own points of interest and individual character. The most expensive area to stay and eat out in is around San Marco. This district and the streets leading to the Rialto Bridge and along the waterfront can get very busy at times.

Without a good map it is easy to get disorientated, although it adds to the fun. For a more relaxed and cheaper option Dorsoduro, with its fine churches and picturesque squares, is a good bet. Many people choose to stay towards Castello, which offers some cheaper small hotels and restaurants.

San Marco and San Giorgio Maggiore

The *sestiere*, or district, of San Marco is the historic heart of Venice, home to Piazza San Marco (St Mark's Square),

SAN MARCO

SAN GIORGIO
MAGGIORE

which in turn is home to the Basilica di San Marco (St Mark's), the city's ancient religious centre, and to the Palazzo Ducale (Doges' Palace), Venice's political focus for over 700 years.

On its northern edge, San Marco also contains the Rialto, the germ of the original city, on whose prominent sandbar the first real settlers created homes, probably in the fifth century. It also contains many of the city's designer stores, as well as the Fenice opera house and many of its leading hotels and restaurants. Its western limits, especially around Campo Santo Stefano, Campo Manin and Campo Sant'Angelo, are much quieter, while across the water the Isola di San Giorgio Maggiore is a tiny world unto itself, with some lovely views.

BASILICA DI SAN MARCO
Best places to see, pages 30–31.

CAFFÈ FLORIAN
This frescoed café has been in business since 1720 and serves some of the most expensive coffee and hot chocolate in the city. But how could you resist sitting at an outside table in the heart and soul of the city, the Piazza di San Marco? When established by Floriano Francesoni it was known as Venezia Trionfante and by the early 1800s was a Venetian favourite, popular with Lord Byron and German poet Goethe.
www.caffeflorian.com

✚ 139 C7 ✉ Piazza San Marco 56 ☎ 041 520 5641 🕐 May–Oct daily 9:30am–midnight; Nov–Apr Thu–Tue 10am–10:30pm 🚤 Vallaresso (San Marco)

CAMPANILE DI SAN MARCO
The bell tower rises 99m (325ft) above the piazza, the tallest building in Venice. The original collapsed in 1902 in a heap of rubble but was rebuilt over the next 10 years. It is entered through the beautiful little loggetta, built in the 16th century by Jacopo Sansovino and restored after it was destroyed in 1902. An internal elevator takes visitors to the gallery surrounding the belfry, which has panoramic views of the city, the lagoon and, on clear days, the Veneto and the Alps.

🚹 139 C8 ✉ Piazza San Marco
☎ 041 522 4064 🕐 Jul–Aug
daily 9–9; Apr–Jun, Sep, Oct
daily 9–7; Nov–Mar daily
9:30–4:15 🖐 Expensive 🚤 San
Zaccaria/Vallaresso (San Marco)

CAMPO SANTO STEFANO

This is one of Venice's finest
squares, busy and popular
but big enough to absorb
the crowds, the local
children, the students and
backpackers who meet up
here. At its north end is the
church of Santo Stefano
(▶ 63), one of the city's
loveliest. There are some
good cafés, with the best
known, Paolin, said to serve
the best ice cream in
Venice. When you relax
here it can be difficult to
visualize it as a former
bullfighting arena, where
oxen were tied to stakes
and baited by dogs, a
practice abandoned in 1802.
🚹 139 C5 🚤 Accademia

CANAL GRANDE

Best places to see,
pages 32–33.

MUSEO CIVICO CORRER

The principal historical museum of the city runs above
the Procuratie Nuove arcade on the west and south
sides of the Piazza and is entered by a wide marble
staircase at the western end. The museum is based on
the 18th-century collection of Teodoro Correr, a Venetian
worthy, and includes superb paintings – with some
exceptional works by the Bellini family – models,
costumes, footwear, books, weapons and armour, much
of it captured from the Turks. Particularly sinister is the lion's
mask *bocca di leone* (letter/mailbox) for written denunciations of
enemies of the state. There are also relics of the *Bucintoro*, the
huge, elaborate ceremonial galley used by the doges. On the first
floor are the striking statues by Antonio Canova (1757–1822). The
focal point is the poignant study of Daedalus and Icarus, showing
the father fixing wings onto his son's arms.

The Correr is part of an ensemble of linked buildings at
the western end of San Marco, which also house the city's
archaelogical collections and the Biblioteca Marciana, creating
one of Venice's biggest and finest museum complexes. The
wonderfully stunning state rooms of the library display
manuscripts and early books beneath the ceiling of allegorical
Mannerist paintings.

www.museiciviciveneziani.it

✚ 139 C7 ✉ Ala Napoleonica, Piazza San Marco ☎ 041 240 5211 or call
centre 041 520 9070 🕒 Apr–Oct daily 9–7; Nov–Mar daily 9–5 ✋ Expensive
but valid for Museo Archeologico Nazionale, Sala Monumnetali della
Biblioteca Marciana and Palazzo Ducale 🚤 Vallaresso (San Marco)

PALAZZO CONTARINI DEL BOVOLO

The Palazzo Contarini del Bovolo can unfortunately only be seen
from the outside. It does, however, have a remarkable spiral
staircase in its open courtyard on the Calle della Vida, close to the
Campo Manin. The Bovolo Staircase (appropriately, *bovolo* means

snail shell in Venetian dialect) is a remarkably delicate feat of architecture and is best seen by moonlight.

🕂 139 B6 ⊠ Calle dei Risi, San Marco ☎ 041 270 2464 🕓 Apr–Oct daily 10–6; Nov–Mar Sat–Sun 10–4 ✋ Moderate 🚢 Rialto

PALAZZO DUCALE

Best places to see, pages 36–37.

PALAZZO GRASSI

This vast classic 18th-century palace has notable frescoes but was much modernized in the 1980s when it was acquired by the Fiat car company and used as an exhibition space. It was bought by the Venice authorities in 2004 and subsequently sold to French billionaire François Pinault, who is to house his suberb art collection in the *palazzo*.

🕂 138 C4 ⊠ Campo San Samuele 🕓 Closed at time of writing; ask at the tourist office 🚢 San Samuele

PIAZZA SAN MARCO
Best places to see, pages 38–39.

PUNTOLAGUNA
This state-of-the-art, multimedia information centre run by Venice's water authority gives information about the canal system and the lagoon, and the work going on to safeguard the future of the city and its buildings.

www.salve.it

✚ 138 C4 ✉ Campo Santo Stefano, San Marco 2949 ☎ 041 529 3582 🕐 Mon–Fri 2:30–5:30 ✋ Free 🚢 Accademia

SAN GIORGIO MAGGIORE
Best places to see, pages 40–41.

SANTA MARIA DELLA FAVA
On a back route from San Marco to the Rialto, the church of Santa Maria della Fava translates as 'St Mary of the Bean' after a popular cake called *fave dolce* (sweet beans) once produced by a nearby bakery and traditionally eaten on All Souls' Day (1 November). The 18th-century church is also known as Santa Maria della Consolazione. It is high-ceilinged and decorated in grey statuary by Bernardi, the teacher of Canova, and has an early painting by Tiepolo, *The Education of the Virgin*. A sombre contrast is the *Madonna and Child* with *St Philip Neri* by Giambattista Piazzetta.

✚ 139 A7 ✉ Campo Rubbi, San Marco ☎ 041 522 4601 🕐 Mon–Sat 8:30–12, 4:30–6:30, Sun 8:30–12 ✋ Free 🚢 Rialto

SANTA MARIA DEL GIGLIO

The carvings on the façade depict fortified cities and warships, commemorating the naval and diplomatic career of Antonio Barbaro, whose family paid for the building of the façade as his monument. The interior contains paintings by Tintoretto.

✚ 139 C5 ✉ Campo Santa Maria del Giglio, San Marco 2452 ☎ 041 275 0462 🕔 Mon–Sat 10–5, Sun 1–5 💶 Inexpensive 🚢 Giglio

SAN MAURIZIO

This faces the square on the well-trodden route between San Marco and the Accademia Bridge, where antiques markets are occasionally held. Rebuilt in 1806, it is a handsome, plain church in neoclassical style. In 2004, it opened as a Vivaldi exhibition centre. The cool and elegant interior now displays a series of exhibits of the life and times of the Venetian composer. You can buy all manner of CDs, tapes and DVDs relating to the composer and you can reserve concert tickets for events at Pietà (► 73).

✚ 139 C5 ✉ Campo San Maurizio, San Marco ☎ 041 241 1840 🕔 Daily 9:30–7:30 💶 Free 🚢 Giglio

SAN MOISÈ

The over-elaborate baroque façade of San Moisè commands the attention of those walking towards San Marco from the Accademia Bridge. Its interior is just as odd: the high altar appears at first sight to be a bizarre rock garden but turns out to be a tableau of *Moses on Mount Sinai Receiving the Tablets*. The building is a startling contrast to the smooth Bauer hotel next door.

✚ 139 C7 ✉ Campo San Moisè, San Marco 1456 ☎ 041 528 5840 🕔 Mon–Sat 10–12 💶 Free 🚢 Vallaresso (San Marco)

a stroll

from San Marco

Start in Piazza San Marco (▶ 38–39), taking in all the sights.

Facing the Basilica take the right-hand corner past the Campanile and the Palazzo Ducale to the waterfront and turn right. Continue along the canal and turn right up Calle Vallaresso. Continue to the intersection and turn left and into Campo San Moisè with the elaborate church of San Moisè (▶ 59). Cross the bridge into Calle Larga XXII Marzo, then bear left at the end and on into Campo Santa Maria del Giglio (▶ 59). Leave the church on your right and bearing right, cross the two bridges into Campo San Maurizio, passing the church of the same name (▶ 59). Continue over the next bridge to Campo Santo Stefano (▶ 55).

This square is one of the loveliest in Venice and good for lunch or just for people-watching.

Pass the church of Santo Stefano (➤ 63) on your right and over the bridge into Campo Sant'Angelo. Follow the canal immediately right to Calle Caotorta, cross the bridge, turn left and follow along the side of the newly restored Teatro la Fenice (➤ 63) out into Campo San Fantin.

Campo San Fantin is a meeting place for theatregoers, and the stunning Fenice hosts superb concerts and operas.

In the left-hand corner of the square take Calle della Verona and continue along, turning right into Calle della Mandola at the end. Proceed over the canal into Campo Manin. Cross the square, taking the left-hand corner into Salizzada San Luca and into the next square, keeping left into Calle San Luca, which takes you into Calle Fabbri, one of the city's major shopping streets. Turn left and then first right. Keep straight on past the church of San Salvador (➤ 62) into Marzarieta Due Aprile. Continue on to San Bartolomeo and turn left to the Ponte di Rialto (Rialto Bridge; ➤ 88).

Distance 2km (1.25 miles)
Time 1 hour plus stops
Start point Piazza San Marco ✚ 139 C7
End point Ponte di Rialto ✚ 139 A7
Lunch Campo Santo Stefano (➤ 55) is a charming, quiet and unspoiled square with several restaurants and cafés, including Paolin, one of the best places for ice cream in the city

SAN SALVADOR

This is regarded as one of the finest and most beautiful
Renaissance churches in Italy and a change from so many
Byzantine and Gothic buildings seen in Venice. It is principally
admired for its internal architecture, and its works of art feature
two paintings by Titian. *The Annunciation* is found at the end of the
right-hand aisle and if you are in any doubt as to the artist, look for
the autograph 'Tizianus, fecit, fecit'. The other, *The Transfiguration*,
hangs over the high altar.

✚ 139 B7 ⊠ Campo San Salvador, San Marco 4826 ☎ 041 523 6717, 041
296 0630 ◉ Mon–Sat 9–12, 3–6/7, Sun 4–7:15 🖐 Free 🚤 Rialto

SANTO STEFANO

This large, handsome church has one of only two 'ship's keel' roofs – like a huge, inverted wooden hull – in the city (the other is in San Giacomo dell'Orio). Richly painted and decorated with inlaid, multi-coloured marble, the high Gothic interior is one of the city's loveliest. It is the only church in Venice to be built directly over a canal. The church contains paintings by Tintoretto, including the highly theatrical *Agony in the Garden* and *Last Supper*. Outside are cloisters and a leaning 16th-century campanile.

✠ 139 C5 ✉ Campo Santo Stefano, San Marco 2774 ☎ 041 522 5061
🎬 Mon–Sat 10–5 👣 Inexpensive 🚢 Accademia/San Samuele

TEATRO LA FENICE

The theatre was utterly destroyed by fire on 29 January 1996. More than a year later two electricians were sentenced for arson, the fire shrouded in mystery. It was not the first time the theatre had been wrecked by fire. Built by Giannantonio Silva in 1792, it had to be rebuilt after a fire in 1836. The most recent, prolonged restoration was well worth waiting for. The new theatre – a wonderful opulent reconstruction in gilt, stucco and marble – surpasses the old. In addition the equipment and sound systems are second to none. You will need to reserve well in advance for performances but you can join a tour to see all its glory.

www.teatrolafenice.org

✠ 139 C6 ✉ Campo San Fantin, San Marco
☎ 041 786 611. Call centre 041 2424 🎬 Tours only;
reserve in advance by person or telephone, fax or
internet. Tours last 45 mins 👣 Tours moderate
🚢 Ca' Rezzonico

TORRE DELL'OROLOGIO

The tower stands above the arch leading to the Mercerie shopping street close to the Basilica di San Marco. Designed by Mauro Codussi and built at the end of the 15th century, its remarkable, brightly enamelled clock face and its digital clock are linked with automata, which attract crowds in the Piazza. The exterior stone dial shows the 24 hours in Roman numerals; the interior face shows signs of the zodiac and phases of the moon. On the summit of the tower two large bronze figures known as the Mori (Moors) strike the hour. During Ascension Week and at Epiphany, figures of the Magi emerge to either side of the clock face and bow to the statue of the Madonna above it. It has reopened following a lengthy restoration begun in 1999.

➕ 139 C8 ✉ Piazza San Marco ⏲ Guided visits in English Mon–Wed at 9, 10, 11, and Thu–Sun at 1, 2, 3 (reservations compulsory – call 041 520 9070) 🛥 Vallaresso (San Marco)/San Zaccaria

Castello

Castello is the most easterly of Venice's six *sestieri*, and one whose many quiet corners, delightful churches and other sights are often overlooked by visitors seduced by the more immediate attractions of nearby San Marco.

Walk to its eastern margins, beyond the Arsenale, Venice's vast former shipyards, and you'll find a very different city, one with few visitors and plenty of working Venetians. Even close to San Marco, in squares around the fine church of San Giovanni in Bragora, or the more distant San Francesco della Vigna, little neighbourhood bars and shops lend the district a different air. Be sure to wander at random, but also to see gems such as Santi Giovanni e Paolo and the Scuola di San Giorgio degli Schiavoni.

ARSENALE

The naval powerhouse of the Venetian Empire was the Arsenale, the great dockyard in the east of the city. Surrounded by 15th-century castellated walls and entered through a monumental archway and watergate, it was where the galleys that conquered the Mediterranean and dominated it for centuries were built and based. The interior is now mostly deserted dockside and bare walls, but the gates – guarded by stone lions brought from Greece in the 17th and 18th centuries – can easily be admired from the *campo* (square) outside.

✚ 141 C7 ✉ Campiello della Malvasia ✋ Moderate
🎦 Arsenale

CAMPO SANTI GIOVANNI E PAOLO

On the San Marco side of the Grand Canal this square in front of the huge church of Santi Giovanni e Paolo (➤ 42–43), is dominated by the remarkable equestrian bronze statue of Bartolomeo Colleoni, a famous Venetian general of the 15th century.

✚ 137 F5 🚢 Fondamenta Nove/Ospedale

CAMPO SANTA MARIA FORMOSA

Campo Santa Maria Formosa, around the church of that name (➤ 73), is busy with market stalls and open-air café tables.

✚ 140 A4 🚢 San Zaccaria/Rialto

GIARDINI PUBBLICI

On the city's eastern fringes in Castello, this garden is a welcome green space after a heavy dose of architectural grandeur. It was created by Napoleon, who oversaw the draining of a stretch of marshland

and the demolition of several convents to generate this shady haven. It is good for a break from the crowds and pleasant for a picnic. You may notice the pavilions partly hidden by the trees. Used in the Biennale, the biennial art and film exhibition held from June to September (➤ 19), these are closed to the public except during the event. The rest is a grassy space dotted with benches and pine trees, with wide views over the lagoon.

✚ 141 E8 (off map) 🖐 Free 🚢 Giardini

MUSEO DIOCESANO D'ARTE SACRA

This tiny but extraordinary museum is a storeroom and restoration centre for works of art from local churches and monasteries. Some are stolen works of art that have been retrieved by the police. It makes for an ever-changing and pleasantly interesting display of sculpture, silverware and other work, with changing exhibitions in the upstairs gallery. The building dates from the 12th to 13th centuries and the museum's main draw is its superb Romanesque cloister, once the focal point of the Benedictine monastery of Sant'Apollonia, the only cloister of this period in the city and a gloriously tranquil place to visit.

✚ 140 C4 ✉ Sant'Apollonia, Castello 4312 ☎ 041 277 0561, 041 522 9166 🕒 Call for latest hours 🖐 Free 🚢 San Zaccaria

MUSEO DELLA FONDAZIONE QUERINI STAMPALIA

The Querini Stampalia *palazzo* was the home of another grand Venetian family and 20 rooms are still furnished with their splendid collection of pictures and furniture, accumulated by aristocrat Giovanni Querini in the 19th century. His foundation specified the opening of a library to promote learning, and it is still used enthusiastically by students today. This and the Palazzo Mocenigo (➤ 87) are two of many such palaces illustrating the richness of Venice at the height of its power.
www.querinistampalia.it

✚ 141 B5 ✉ Campiello Querini Stampalia, Castello ☎ 041 271 1411
🕐 Tue–Sun 10–6 ✋ Moderate 🚤 San Zaccaria

MUSEO STORICO NAVALE

The Naval Museum records the illustrious maritime past of Venice with a magnificent collection of ship models, pictures and relics housed in an old granary near the Arsenale (➤ 66), which was the naval base of the Republic. The exhibits range from models of the galleys that fought the corsairs and Turks to the human torpedoes used in World War II. There is a special section devoted to the gondola and other Venetian craft, with actual boats displayed in part of the Arsenale itself.

✚ 141 D8 ✉ Campo San Biagio, Castello 2148 ☎ 041 520 0276
🕐 Mon–Fri 8:45–1:30, Sat 8:45–1 ✋ Inexpensive 🚤 Arsenale

RIVA DEGLI SCHIAVONI

The Riva degli Schiavoni, or 'The Waterfront of the Slavs', is the principal waterside promenade of Venice, running eastwards from the Doges' Palace to the Ca' di Dio canal, where its name changes and then continuing to the Giardini (public gardens). After the Doges' Palace and the adjoining State Prison comes the Danieli and a succession of other grand hotels facing the Basin of San

Marco. The wide, paved Riva, broken by a succession of bridges over canals, is cluttered with café tables and souvenir-sellers' stalls at its western end, while its waterside is busy with *vaporetto* piers and the pleasure boats and tugs that moor there. Leading from the Riva to the north are many alleys and archways running into the maze of the city and to a few squares, notably the Campo San Zaccaria and the Campo Bandiera e Moro.

➕ 141 C5 🏛 San Zaccaria

SAN FRANCESCO DELLA VIGNA

This superb Palladian church, one of Venice's best kept secrets, is in the less-visited northeast of the city near the Arsenale, and its huge campanile is sometimes mistaken for that of San Marco from a distance. It contains beautiful paintings – although none of the first rank – including a delightful 15th-century *Madonna and Child Enthroned* by Antonio da Negroponte.

➕ 141 A7 ✉ Campo di San Francesco, Castello 2786 ☎ 041 520 6102
🕐 Irregular hours ♿ Free ⛴ Ospedale/Celestia

a walk to the gardens of Castello

Start at the Palazzo Ducale on the edge of San Marco and turn left onto Riva degli Schiavoni. As you go over the first bridge look to the left to see the renowned Ponte dei Sospiri (Bridge of Sighs). Continuing along you can see the famous Danieli hotel – named after its first proprietor Dal Niel – before crossing the next bridge. Housed in a former 15th-century *palazzo* it has been a hotel since the early 19th century, its interior retaining many of the original features. At this point out across the water is the Isola di San Giorgio Maggiore, with its striking church (➤ 40–41).

Carry on along the waterfront, pausing to look back over your shoulder at the superb view. Go over the next bridge and past the church of La Pietà (➤ 73). Continue over two more bridges and go past the Arsenale vaporetto stop and over the next bridge into Campo San Biagio with the Museo Storico Navale (➤ 68). Continue along Riva dei Sette Martiri as far as the Giardini Pubblici (➤ 66–67). After the Giardini vaporetto stop turn left into the gardens where you will see the Biennale Internazionale d'Arte in front of you. Turn left and keep bearing left until first right takes you into Viale Garibaldi with the Garibaldi monument at the end. Go through the impressive gates at the end and turn left into Via Giuseppe Garibaldi.

This vibrant street is in the heart of working-class Castello, where you will feel a long way from the popular narrow streets and canals of the tourist trail.

About 150m (163yds) on the right take the narrow alley Calle del Forno, crossing the bridge at the end. Turn left and at the canal turn right to the Arsenale (▶ 66). Cross the bridge and keep on to the church of San Martino (▶ 74). Go around the church and continue with the canal on your right until you reach Calle della Pegola. Turn down here and at the end turn right into Calle dei Forni, which takes you back to the waterfront. The Arsenale vaporetto stop is almost right in front of you.

Distance 3.5km (2 miles)
Time 2 hours plus stops
Start point Palazzo Ducale ✚ 139 C8
End point Arsenale *vaporetto* stop ✚ 141 C7
Lunch Take a refreshment stop among the locals at Via Giuseppe Garibaldi

SAN GIORGIO DEI GRECI

The church is recognizable by its tilted 16th-century campanile, caused by subsidence. The church of the Greek community, many of whom fled Constantinople when it was taken by the Turks in the 15th century, has Byzantine and Greek Orthodox decoration.

✚ 141 B6 ✉ Fondamenta dei Greci, Castello 3412 ☎ 041 522 6581 🕐 Mon, Wed–Sat 9–12:30, 2:30–4:30, Sun 9–1 💷 Inexpensive 🚤 San Zaccaria

SAN GIOVANNI IN BRAGORA

This fascinating little parish church, where Antonio Vivaldi was baptized, lies hidden in a quiet campo off the Riva degli Schiavoni, and a plaque outside records the date of the baptism as 6 May, 1678. Among the paintings in the church is a lovely, peaceful

Madonna and Child with Saints by Bartolomeo Vivarini. Over the high altar there is another highlight, the painting of the *Baptism of Christ* (1492) by Cima da Conegliano.

✚ 141 C6 ✉ Campo Bandiera e Moro, Castello 3790 ☎ 041 296 0630 🕐 Mon–Sat 9–11, 3:30–5:30 💷 Free 🚌 Arsenale

SANTI GIOVANNI E PAOLO
Best places to see, pages 42–43.

SANTA MARIA FORMOSA
The 15th-century church dominates a large square enlivened by cafés and market stalls. Designed by Mauro Codussi in 1492, it was revamped according to Renaissance ideals while retaining its original Byzantine plan. The dome was destroyed by a bomb in 1916 but was

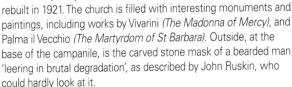

rebuilt in 1921. The church is filled with interesting monuments and paintings, including works by Vivarini *(The Madonna of Mercy)*, and Palma il Vecchio *(The Martyrdom of St Barbara)*. Outside, at the base of the campanile, is the carved stone mask of a bearded man 'leering in brutal degradation', as described by John Ruskin, who could hardly look at it.

✚ 140 A4 ✉ Campo Santa Maria Formosa, Castello ☎ 041 523 4645, 041 275 0462 🕐 Mon–Sat 10–5, Sun 1–5 💷 Inexpensive 🚌 San Zaccaria

SANTA MARIA DELLA VISITAZIONE (LA PIETÀ)
This has been used for concerts since the 17th century, and during the 18th century Vivaldi composed music for the choir. Music is still played here regularly, when audiences can admire the oval painting by Giambattista Tiepolo on the ceiling, *The Coronation of the Virgin*. The church is only opened for concerts.
www.vivaldi.it

✚ 141 C6 ✉ Riva degli Schiavoni, Castello ☎ 041 523 1096 🕐 Varies for concerts 💷 Varies for concerts 🚌 San Zaccaria

SAN MARTINO

This is a lovely, little-visited church near the Arsenale, and it is probable that the wooden angels and cherubs around the organ were carved by craftsmen who decorated the great galleys in the dockyard. It has another spectacular ceiling painted with an *Ascension into Heaven*, past the pillars of an atrium, that seems to grow out of the architecture. The profusion of monuments and paintings makes this a very Venetian church, and outside in the wall is one of the now rare 'lion's mask' letter boxes (mailboxes) for notes that decounce enemies of the state.

✚ 141 C7 ✉ Campo San Martino, Castello 2298 ◷ Irregular hours ✋ Free 🚲 Arsenale

SAN PIETRO DI CASTELLO

As it stands forlornly on its little island at the far eastern extremity of Venice, the church seems to be dreaming of past glories. This was the first of the central Venetian islands to be settled, and the church became the cathedral of Venice in AD775, remaining so until 1807, when the Basilica di San Marco, formerly the Doges' private chapel, took its place. Its isolation here throughout the life of the Venetian Republic was a deliberate attempt to minimize the influence of the Pope and Rome. It overlooks a usually deserted stretch of grass and trees. Inside, the church, which was built to a Palladian design in the 16th century, is lofty and rather grand but, above all, neglected.

✚ 141 E8 (off map) ✉ Campo San Pietro, Isola di San Pietro ☎ 041 523 8950 ◷ Irregular hours ✋ Inexpensive 🚲 Giardini

SAN ZACCARIA

The massive 16th-century church – with traces of its predecessors – is filled with paintings. The most celebrated of these is Bellini's *Madonna and Four Saints* (1505) in the second chapel on the left. During the Venetian Republic, the nunnery attached to the church was favoured by rich families as a refuge for their unattached

daughters. There is also a permanently waterlogged crypt where eight early doges are interred.

✚ 141 C5 ✉ Campo San Zaccaria, Castello 4963 ☎ 041 522 1257 🕐 Mon–Sat 10–12, 4–6, Sun 11–12, 4–6 💰 Free; inexpensive to chapels, sacristy and crypt 🚤 San Zaccaria

SCUOLA GRANDE DI SAN MARCO

Another magnificent *scuola* with a fine exterior stands next to the church of Santi Giovanni e Paolo and now houses the main hospital and can be visited by appointment only. Its most interesting works of art, relief carvings incoporating startling perspectives, can be seen on the outside wall facing the *campo*.

✚ 137 E5 ✉ San Giovanni e Paolo, Castello 🚤 Ospedale Civile

SCUOLA DI SAN GIORGIO DEGLI SCHIAVONI

This tiny, intimate building was set up in 1451 to look after the interests of Venice's Dalmatian, or Slav, population, formerly slaves but by the 15th century established as merchants and sailors. The *scuola* has the early 16th-century Vittore Carpaccio's paintings as its main attraction, an enchanting frieze illustrating the lives of three Dalmatian saints: St George, St Jerome and St Tryphon. This cycle of paintings can be found on the upper part of the walls in the ground floor hall. Ranged below one of the most lavish of ceilings, the cycle begins with the story of *St George Slaying the Dragon*, an exceptionally graphic and detailed painting, followed by the *Triumph of St George, St George Baptizing the Gentiles* and the *Miracle of St Tryphon*. The next two, the *Agony in the Garden* and the *Calling of St Matthew*, precede three works concerning the life of St Jerome, the best-loved being *St Augustine in his Study* at the moment of Jerome's death – an intimate glimpse into a medieval Venetian study, complete with appealing dog.

✚ 141 B6 ✉ Calle Furlani, Castello 3259A ☎ 041 522 8828 ◉ Apr–Oct Tue–Sat 9:30–12:30, 3:30–6:30, Sun 9:30–12:30; Nov–Mar Tue–Sat 10–12:30, 3–6, Sun 10–12:30 ◍ Inexpensive ⛴ San Zaccaria/Arsenale

CANNAREGIO

Cannaregio

Most visitors have only a fleeting acquaintance with Cannaregio, the *sestiere* that embraces much of northern Venice, passing swiftly through it as they walk or take a boat from the railway station to Piazza San Marco. Yet its many quiet corners and distinctive areas, such as the old Jewish ghetto, are some of Venice's most seductive and unvisited.

Here, as in Castello, you are often a long way from the hordes, but – as ever in Venice – only moments from beautiful buildings, pretty squares and sudden, unexpected views. Madonna dell'Orto is the loveliest church and the Ca' d'Oro the most tempting museum, but don't overlook the old ghetto's fascinating Museo Ebraico or the tucked-away churches of San Giobbe and Sant'Alvise.

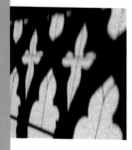

CA' D'ORO

The 'House of Gold', the most famous *palazzo* on the Grand Canal, was named after the gilding on its elaborate exterior when it was new. Inside the *palazzo* an elegant new gallery displays Italian art, including frescoes by Titian and Giorgione. Reopened in 1984, this magnificent building retains its architectural bones, but sadly not its atmosphere of former grandeur. You can get a really good view of the *palazzo* from the opposite side of the Grand Canal at the Pescheria (fish market).
www.cadoro.org

✚ 136 E3 ✉ Calle di Ca' d'Oro, Cannaregio 3932 ☎ 041 523 8790
🕐 Mon 8:15–2, Tue–Sun 8:15–7:15 👆 Moderate 🚤 Ca' d'Oro

CAMPO DEI MORI

This is one of the quieter squares in the city, off the tourist trail in Cannaregio, and a lovely spot for an ice cream, a coffee or a drink in one of the little friendly bars. You can mingle with the locals and watch the world go by. It is also close to two of the finest churches in the city, Sant'Alvise (➤ 81) and Madonna dell'Orto (➤ 80). It gives you an insight into real Venetian street life, away from the masses.

✚ 135 B6 🚤 Orto

GESUITI (SANTA MARIA ASSUNTA)

The early 18th-century Jesuits built their church to impress, and the statuary along the skyline of its pediment gives a hint of what is within. Inside, the pillars and floor seem to be hung with green and white damask silk, which is also draped and ruffled around the pulpit on the north wall, but it all turns out to be marble.

✚ 137 D5 ✉ Campo dei Gesuiti, Cannaregio 4885 ☎ 041 528 6579
🕐 Daily 10–12, 3–6 👆 Free 🚤 Fondamenta Nove

IL GHETTO

This is a small district enclosed by canals in the northwest of the city and not far from the rail station. It was named after a 14th-century cannon-casting foundry, or *geto* in Venetian – the name was subsequently given to Jewish enclaves the world over. Since Jews were only permitted to live in this small area from 1516 to 1797, they were allowed to build higher houses than elsewhere in the city and so the buildings rise to eight floors.

The main approach to the Ghetto is through a narrow alley leading off the Fondamenta di Cannaregio. This brings you to the Ghetto Vecchio and over a bridge to the Campo Ghetto Nuovo, a separate island that's the heart of the Ghetto and where you will find the Holocaust Memorial, a series of seven reliefs by Arbit Blatas, commemorating the deportation and extermination of the city's Jews, and the **Museo Ebraico.** The museum opened in 1955 and displays a collection of religious objects, prayer books, textiles, documents and silverware.

Today the area remains the focus for the religion, and there are still a small number of Jewish families living in the Ghetto, with two synagogues in regular use.

www.ghetto.it; **www**.museoebraico.it

➕ 134 C4 🚊 Guglie

Museo Ebraico

✉ Campo del Ghetto Nuovo 2902B ☎ 041 715 359
🕐 Jun–Sep Sun–Fri 10–7, Oct–May Sun–Fri 10–5:30. May close early on Fri 🦽 Inexpensive

MADONNA DELL'ORTO

Isolated in the north of the city in Cannaregio, the church is a good goal for a long walk. It was magnificently restored after the flood of 1966 by funds raised in Britain. Spend a few minutes to admire the mainly Gothic façade before entering the church. The windows are obviously Gothic, the onion-shaped dome echoes the earlier Byzantine style, while its elegant doorway is clearly Renaissance.

The simple interior, with its sense of space, height and light, is laid out in basilica form. Tintoretto, who is buried in one of the side chapels – you can see his tomb – was a parishioner and painted some superb pictures as a gift to the church. In the chancel are the magnificent *Last Judgement* and *The Making of the Golden Calf*. Look for the charming *Presentation of the Virgin* at the end of the right nave above the door. In the apse there are further paintings by Tintoretto, the *Beheading of St Paul* and *St Peter's Vision of the Cross*, full of movement and pathos. Other great works include Cima da Conegliano's *St John the Baptist*.

The church gained its name from the story of a statue of the Madonna and Child found in a local vegetable garden or *orto*, and believed to have worked miracles. The statue is in the Cappella di San Mauro off the end of the right aisle near the main altar.

🔢 135 B6 ✉ Campo della Madonna dell'Orto, Cannaregio 3520 ☎ 041 719 933 🕐 Mon–Sat 10–5 💶 Inexpensive 🚏 Orto

PALAZZO LABIA

Palazzo Labia, not far from the Santa Lucia rail station, is now the headquarters of the Italian broadcasting service, RAI. It contains one of the loveliest rooms in Venice, decorated by the elder Tiepolo with gloriously coloured frescoes of Antony and Cleopatra in 16th-century dress and dramatic perspectives.

🔢 134 D4 ✉ Campo San Geremia ☎ 041 524 2812, 041 781 277 🕐 Call for latest hours 💶 Call to inquire 🚏 Guglie

SANT'ALVISE

Although one of the most remote churches in the city, this is a useful destination for a long walk including the Madonna dell'Orto (► opposite) and the Ghetto (► 79). Its most notable painting (by Tiepolo) was removed to the Gallerie dell'Accademia, and the church's principal feature is now a spectacular but rather clumsily executed painted trompe l'oeil ceiling, depicting Heaven as seen from a grandiose courtyard. This is a somewhat cruder version of the extraordinary painted ceiling in San Pantalon (► 90).

⊹ 135 B5 ⊠ Campo Sant'Alvise, Canneregio ☎ 041 524 4664, 041 275 0462 ◑ Mon–Sat 10–5 ⑰ Inexpensive ➡ Sant'Alvise

SANTI APOSTOLI

There has been a church on this site since the 9th century, and the present 16th-century church incorporates some parts of the early building, with the interior reflecting some 18th-century additions. The church is worth visiting just for *The Communion of Santa Lucia* by the elder Tiepolo in the delightful 15th-century Corner family chapel. The exceptionally tall 17th-century campanile, crowned by an onion dome, is a well-known Venetian landmark.

⊹ 136 E4 ⊠ Campo dei Santi Apostoli, Canneregio 4542 ☎ 041 523 8297 ◑ Mon–Sat 7:30–11:30, 5–7, Sun 8:30–12, 4.15–6:30 ⑰ Free ➡ Ca' d'Oro

SAN GEREMIA E LUCIA

Standing on the corner of the Grand Canal and the Canale di Cannaregio, this vast, light, plain church, originally dedicated solely to St Jerome, is now remarkable for housing the mummified body of St Lucia, which was removed from her own church when it was demolished to make way for the rail station that was to be named after her. Wearing a gold mask and a red and gold robe, she lies in a glass case.

✚ 134 D4 ✉ Campo San Geremia, Cannaregio 334 🕐 Mon–Fri 8:30–12, 3:30–6:30, Sun 9:30–12, 5:30–6:30 ✋ Free ⛴ San Marcuola/Ferrovia

SAN GIOBBE

San Giobbe is another remote church in the northwest of the city that is often locked. Dedicated to the Old Testament figure Job, it is worth a visit to see those of its paintings that have not been removed to the Gallerie dell'Accademia, including a triptych by Antonio Vivarini. It is currently being restored.

✚ 134 C2 ✉ Campo San Giobbe, Cannaregio 620 ☎ 041 275 0462 🕐 Mon–Sat 10–5 ✋ Inexpensive ⛴ Ponte dei Tre Archi

SAN GIOVANNI CRISOSTOMO

Just a few minutes' walk north from the Rialto is San Giovanni Crisostomo, literally St John the Golden-Tongued, a small, busy, Venetian parish church and an excellent example of Renaissance architecture. Its architect, the Renaissance master Mauro Codussi, based his design around the Greek cross form. Richly decorated, it is remarkable for a lovely painting showing *Saints Jerome, Christopher and Louis of Toulouse* by Giovanni Bellini.

🛂 136 F4 ✉ Campo San Giovanni Crisostomo, Cannaregio 5889 ☎ 041 520 5906 🕔 Irregular hours 👖 Free 🚤 Rialto

SANTA MARIA DEI MIRACOLI

One of the most exquisite small buildings in Venice, this church has often been described as looking like a jewel box. Built in the 15th century of softly coloured marble, it stands beside a canal with such elegance that its design needs no embellishment to satisfy the eye. When closed, the outer doors are often left open so that the interior, which is as lovely as the exterior, can be admired through an inner glass door.

Have a good look around the outside before venturing in. The church was built to house an image of the Virgin painted in 1409 by Nicolò di Pietro, which had been placed in a street shrine. The image became exceedingly popular and credited with miraculous powers, and Pietro Lombardo was commissioned to build the church, a Renaissance triumph.

Inside, the marble theme continues in brilliant tones, with some of the most wonderfully intricate carving to be found in any church in the city. Lombardo and his sons, Tullio and Antonio, executed an array of beautifully sculpted saints leading to the raised choir. Look up to admire the striking ceiling, covered with 50 *Saints and Prophets* (1528) by Pier Pennacchi. The church is understandably a popular wedding venue.

🛂 137 E5 🕔 Campo dei Miracoli, Cannaregio 6075 ☎ 041 275 0462 🕔 Mon–Sat 10–5 👖 Inexpensive 🚤 Ca d'Oro/Rialto

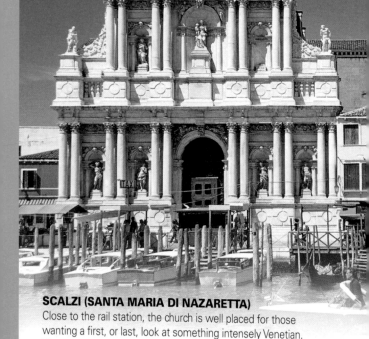

SCALZI (SANTA MARIA DI NAZARETTA)

Close to the rail station, the church is well placed for those
wanting a first, or last, look at something intensely Venetian.
The *scalzi* were 'barefooted' Carmelite friars who came here in
the mid-17th century and commissioned the church. The ornate
baroque façade is an indication of the sumptuous but gloomy
interior of multi-coloured marble, statuary and 18th-century
paintings. Appropriately, the last of the doges, Ludovico Manin,
is buried there.

✚ 134 D3 ✉ Fondamenta Scalzi, Cannaregio ☎ 041 715 115 ⏰ Daily
8–12:50, 4–6:50 💲 Free 🚊 Ferrovia

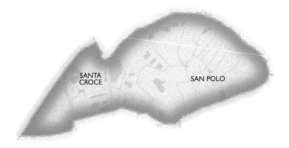

SANTA
CROCE

SAN POLO

San Polo and Santa Croce

San Polo and Santa Croce make up much of central and western Venice, two large and ill-defined districts contained within the great curve of the Grand Canal.

San Polo, to the east, contains the better-known sights, notably the wonderful Rialto markets and Santa Maria Gloriosa dei Frari, Venice's largest church and most captivating religious building after

San Marco. Here, too, is the Scuola Grande di San Rocco, the most important of Venice's *scuole* (charitable foundations), which is also a shrine to the work of Tintoretto, one of the city's leading artists.

Santa Croce is altogether more peaceful, typified by venerable churches such as San Stae and San Giacomo dell'Orio and its sleepy square, and home to a handful of pleasant cafés and restaurants.

CA' PESARO

It's worth visiting if only to see inside this enormous 17th-century restored baroque *palazzo* overlooking the Grand Canal. It was built for Giovanni Pesaro, who became Doge in 1685, and now houses contemporary art exhibitions on the first two floors and Oriental art on the top floor. The Museo d'Arte Moderna was founded in 1902 with a handful of pedestrian pieces bought from the Biennale. The Museo d'Arte Orientale has a wealth of objects collected by Conti di Bardi during a trip to the Far East in the 19th century.

www.museiciviveneziani.it

⊞ 135 E6 ⊠ Fondamenta Ca' Pesaro, Santa Croce ☎ Palace and museums 041 524 0662 🕔 Palace and museums Apr–Oct Tue–Sun 10–6; Nov–Mar Tue–Sun 10–5 ✋ Moderate, includes admission to palace and museums 🛳 San Stae

CAMPO SAN POLO

On the other side of the Grand Canal, the largest square is Campo San Polo, where the huge marble wellhead is a gathering place for the young on summer evenings.

⊞ 139 A5 🛳 San Silvestro

MERCATO DI RIALTO

The oldest market in the Rialto is the fish market, located on the same site

for over a thousand years. Today it is housed in and around the lovely vaulted neo-Gothic Pescheria. Get here early before the crowds for the best atmosphere. Next to this is an array of fruit and vegetable stalls. The produce may have been shipped from the mainland, but its quality and taste are second to none. The prices are pretty good, too. The original traders and merchants lived in the warren of streets around here, which are bursting with butchers, bakers and purveyors of all kinds of foods.

➕ 135 F7 ✉ Rialto 🕓 Mon–Sat 8–1; fish market is closed on Mon
🚢 Rialto

PALAZZO MOCENIGO

This was the home of one of the oldest and grandest Venetian families until recent years. The nine elegantly furnished rooms of the 17th-century *palazzo* provide a rare insight into 18th-century Venetian noble life. Richly gilded and painted, these rooms, with their fine furniture and Murano glass chandeliers, still have a private feeling about them. Many of the paintings, friezes and frescoes are by Jacopo Guarana. The building also houses a library and a collection of period costume, together with a small exhibition of antique Venetian textiles.

➕ 135 E5 ✉ Salizzada San Stae, Santa Croce 1992 ☎ 041 721 798
🕓 Apr–Oct Tue–Sun 10–5; Nov–Mar Tue–Sun 10–4 ✋ Moderate
🚢 San Stae

PONTE DI RIALTO

Built of Istrian stone in the late 16th century, this was, until
1854, when the Ponte dell'Accademia was completed, the only
crossing of the Grand Canal and replaced an earlier wooden
bridge. A single span, decorated with relief carvings and
balustrades, it is famous for its parallel rows of shops facing
one another on either side of the central path. These sell mostly
jewellery, leather goods, silk and shoes. The bridge commands
fine views of the canal, particularly in the direction of San Marco.

➕ 139 A7 ✉ Canal Grande 🚤 Rialto

SAN CASSIANO

This sumptuous church, with its pillars draped in crimson and an
attractive 13th-century campanile, is worth visiting for Tintoretto's
majestic *Crucifixion* (1565–1568). The other two paintings by the
artist have been heavily restored.

➕ 135 E6 ✉ Campo San Cassiano, San Polo 1852 ☎ 041 721 408
🕐 Apr–Sep daily 10–12, 5:30–7; Oct–Mar daily 10–12, 4:30–6 ✋ Free
🚤 San Stae/Rialto

SAN GIACOMO DELL'ORIO

This busy parish church is in a quiet *campo* in the west of the city, where the only visitors are likely to be those walking to the Piazzale Roma to catch a bus. Its architecture and decoration reflect the growth of Venice: pillars from Byzantium and one of the two 'ship's keel' roofs (like an inverted wooden ship) in Venice – the other is in Santo Stefano (➤ 63); paintings by Venetian masters; and, in comic contrast, a funny little relief carving of a knight – almost a cartoon character – on the outside wall.

🚌 134 E4 ✉ Campo San Giacomo dell'Orio, Santa Croce ☎ 041 275 0462
🕐 Mon–Sat 10–5, Sun 1–5 ✋ Inexpensive 🚤 San Stae/Riva di Biasio

SAN GIACOMO DI RIALTO

Among the fruit and vegetable market stalls at the foot of the Rialto Bridge, this the oldest church in the city – said to have been founded in the early 5th century. It has grown many architectural and decorative curiosities, including a rare brick dome; over-large baroque altarpieces; and a large, 15th-century 24-hour clock on the façade. The church faces the market square, which was once used by bankers, money changers and insurance brokers.

🚌 135 F7 ✉ Campo San Giacomo, San Polo 🕐 Mon–Sat 7–12, 3–6 ✋ Free
🚤 Rialto

SANTA MARIA GLORIOSA DEI FRARI

Best places to see, pages 44–45.

SAN NICOLÒ DA TOLENTINO

This colossal church with a vast, pillared Corinthian portico is close to the Piazzale Roma and is popular for weddings. Embedded in the exterior (under the porch) you can see a cannon ball, left by the Austrians during the siege of 1849. Inside, the church is elaborate, enriched with sculpture and paintings.

🚌 138 A2 ✉ Campo dei Tolentini, Santa Croce 265 ☎ 041 522 2160
🕐 Irregular hours ✋ Free 🚤 Piazzale Roma

SAN PANTALON

This typically Venetian baroque church probably makes a more immediate impact on the visitor than any church in Venice. On entering and looking up, the vast flat ceiling is painted with one enormous view of a mass ascent into Heaven. This startling scene also includes the life and martyrdom of San Pantalon and was painted at the end of the 17th century and the beginning of the 18th. A typically quirky Venetian postscript is the fate of the artist, Gian Antonio Fumiani, who, as he completed his work, stepped back to admire it better, fell from the scaffolding to his death and was buried in the church he had decorated so memorably. The church also contains smaller works by Veronese and Vivarini. Like several other Venetian churches, it has no façade as its builders ran out of money.

✠ 138 B3 ✉ Campo San Pantalon, San polo ☎ 041 523 5893 ◷ Mon–Sat 3–6 ✋ Free 🚤 San Tomà

SAN POLO

The church stands in the largest square after San Marco. Its works of art include fine bronze statues of saints on the high altar and notable paintings by Tintoretto and both Tiepolos, including 18 paintings of The Stations of the Cross by the younger Tiepolo.

🚏 139 A5 ✉ Campo San Polo, San Polo 2102 ☎ 041 275 0462 🕐 Mon–Sat 9–6 💷 Inexpensive 🚤 San Silvestro/San Tomà

SAN STAE

Despite its handsome interior, this church is at its best viewed from the outside. Its neoclassical façade, decorated with joyous baroque statuary, provides one of the most striking views on the Grand Canal. Inside the finest paintings are Tiepolo's *Martyrdom of St Bartholomew* and Piazzetta's *Martyrdom of St James the Great*. The church is used for art exhibitions and concerts.

🚏 135 D6 ✉ Campo San Stae, Canal Grande, Santa Croce 1981 ☎ 041 275 0462 🕐 Mon–Sat 10–5 💷 Inexpensive 🚤 San Stae

SCUOLA GRANDE DI SAN GIOVANNI EVANGELISTA

One of the six Scuole Grande and not generally open to the public but it is worth a visit for its splendid exterior. Located in a tiny square near the Frari, a beautiful Renaissance complex, it was designed by Mauro Codussi in 1454 and has a stunning archway designed by Pietro Lombardo in 1481. The eagle crowning the arch is the symbol of St John the Evangelist. The interior is remarkable for a converging double staircase that leads to the Albergo, the main conference room, hung with scenes from the life of St John. Admission to the building is possible when exhibitions or concerts are being held or sometimes on request.

🚏 134 F4 ✉ Campiello de la Scuola, San Polo ☎ 041 718 8234 🕐 Occasionally open Mon–Sat 10–12, 3–5 💷 Donation 🚤 San Tomà

SCUOLA GRANDE DI SAN ROCCO

Best places to see, pages 48–49.

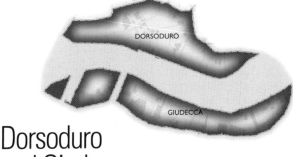

DORSODURO

GIUDECCA

Dorsoduro and Giudecca

Dorsoduro is the most easily identified of Venice's six *sestieri*, the arm of land that curves around the southern edge of the Grand Canal. A largely prosperous residential district, it contains the city's two principal art galleries – the Collezione Peggy Guggenheim, a private collection of modern art, and the Gallerie dell'Accademia, filled with the city's finest paintings from over 500 years.

Also here is the great church of the Salute, one of the distinctive landmarks of the Grand Canal and the centrepiece of the view from San Marco and the Accademia bridge. Dorsoduro, as ever in Venice, is a lovely place to walk, with some particularly fine views from the Zattere, its southern waterfront. Among other things, you'll see La Giudecca, a long narrow island immediately across the water. Once a mostly working-class area, the island is now becoming increasingly chic.

ANGELO RAFFAELE

This church, one of the city's oldest foundations, is located in a secluded part of Dorsoduro. It is notable for its 18th-century organ decorated with paintings by Guardi.

 138 C1 ✉ Campo Angelo Raffaele ☎ 041 522 8548 ⊘ Daily 9–12, 3–5 🖐 Free 🚤 San Basilio

CA' REZZONICO

This immensely grand 17th-century palace overlooking the Grand Canal has been filled with furniture and paintings of the 18th century. The magnificent rooms of the piano nobile (main floor) are richly decorated with gilding, frescoes and painted ceilings, including one by Tiepolo. On the floor above you can see paintings of Venetian life by Guardi and Longhi as well as a succession of small rooms, decorated with frescoes by the younger Tiepolo. The top floor, which houses a collection of costumes, the stock of a pharmacist's shop and a marionette theatre, is often closed.

The poet Robert Browning occupied a suite of rooms below the *piano nobile* (not open to the public) from 1888 until his death here in 1889.

www.museiciviciveneziani.it

🖈 138 C3 ✉ Fondamenta Rezzonico, Dorsoduro 3136 ☎ 041 241 0100 ⊘ Apr–Oct Wed–Mon 10–6; Nov–Mar Wed–Mon 10–5 (ticket office closes 1 hour earlier) 🖐 Expensive 🚤 Ca' Rezzonico

CAMPO SAN BARNABA

Perhaps the most charmingly Venetian of all the squares is the Campo San Barnaba near the Accademia Gallery. Presided over by the noble façade of the church of San Barnaba (a simple parish church with an air of tranquillity) this *campo* bustles with life: shops, two cafés with tables outside and a barge selling the world's most photographed fruit and vegetables moored in the canal that connects with the Grand Canal.

➕ 138 C3 🚤 Ca' Rezzonico

CAMPO SANTA MARGHERITA

More lively is the Campo Santa Margherita, where vendors sell fruit, vegetables, fish and shoes, and local Venetian life goes on undisturbed by crowds of tourists.

➕ 138 B2 🚤 Ca' Rezzonico

COLLEZIONE PEGGY GUGGENHEIM

The collection of Cubist, Abstract and Surrealist art acquired by the late Peggy Guggenheim, the American millionairess, is housed in her former home, an unfinished 18th-century *palazzo* on the Canal Grande, Palazzo Venier de Leoni. This is the perfect antidote to a superfluity of Byzantine, Gothic Renaissance and baroque art. Paintings and sculptures of the 20th century – including Peggy Guggenheim's own discovery, the energetic Jackson Pollock – will delight those who appreciate modern art, while those who do not will enjoy the view from the garden, overlooking the Grand Canal. This is one of the world's most important 20th-century collections outside the US.

www.guggenheim-venice.it

➕ 139 D5 ✉ Calle San Cristoforo, Dorsoduro 701 ☎ 041 240 5411
🕐 Apr–Oct Wed–Mon 10–6; Nov–Mar Wed–Mon 10–6 💷 Expensive
🚣 Accademia/Salute

DOGANA DI MARE

This stands where the Dorsoduro district of Venice (to the east of the church of the Salute ➤ 46–47) juts out like a ship's prow into the lagoon at the junction of the Canal Grande and the Basin of San Marco. On top of its tower stand two bronze figures of Atlas holding up a golden globe surmounted by a figure of Fortune as a wind vane. Behind the tower are the 17th-century Customs warehouses. You can stop for a moment and enjoy the views of San Marco and over the lagoon.

➕ 139 D7 ✉ Dorsoduro 🕐 Closed to the public except during exhibitions
🚣 Salute

GALLERIE DELL'ACCADEMIA

Best places to see, pages 34–35.

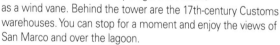

PEGGY
GUGGENHEIM
COLLECTION

GESUATI

Also known as Santa Maria del Rosario, the Gesuati takes its popular name from a religious order of the same name founded at the end of the 14th century, but suppressed in 1688. The order built a small oratory on the site, later adapted and enlarged by the Dominicans into the present church (consecrated in 1736). Its artistic highlights are three ceiling frescoes by Giambattista Tiepolo, depicting scenes from the story of the Dominican order (1737–39).

www.chorusvenezia.org

✚ 138 E3 ✉ Fondamenta delle Zattere ai Gesuati, Dorsoduro 917 ☎ 041 275 0462, 041 523 0625 🕐 Mon–Sat 10–5 💲 Inexpensive 🚏 Zattere

GIUDECCA

The island of the Giudecca lies to the south of central Venice across the wide, deep-water Canale della Giudecca. Originally a chain of small islands, it was settled by a small Jewish community, which lived here until the establishment of the Ghetto (➤ 79). It has always been a popular place to escape the summer heat, even as early as the 13th century when wealthy aristocrats built splendid palaces surrounded by gardens. Subsequently in the 19th and 20th centuries it became an industralized area with the creation of factories and shipyards. This has declined over the last 50 years and today it is primarily a residential area. The main sights are on the north side of the island, including the Redentore (➤ 103), the Zittelle and Sant'Eufemia churches. Here you will also find bars and restaurants, food shops and examples of 14th-century *palazzi*.

➕ 138 F2 🚤 Palanca/Redentore/Zitelle

a walk around Dorsoduro

Start on the south side of the bridge, facing the Gallerie dell'Accademia (▶ 34–35). Turn left into Rio Terrà Antonio Foscarini and continue to the waterfront, passing the church of the Gesuati with ceiling and altar paintings by Tiepolo.

Turn right at the end along the Zattere, turning right just before the bridge. Continue along by the canal. On your left is the boatyard of Squero di San Trovaso (▶ 106) and the church of the same name (▶ 105). Take a left at the second bridge into Calle Toletta and continue straight on crossing another bridge into Campo San Barnaba

(▶ 95). Take the left corner out of the square, cross the first bridge into Rio Terrà Canal and turn left into Sant' Aponal. Turn right into Campo Santa Margherita.

This square is a pleasant place to stop for lunch or a rest.

Return to Sant' Aponal and continue along, turning right by the Scuola Grande (▶ 105) and the church of Santa Maria dei Carmini (▶ 103). Continue by the canal

and cross the fourth bridge past the church of San Sebastiano (▶ 104–105) on your left. Continue ahead across Campazza San Sebastiano to go behind the church of Angelo Raffaele (▶ 94). Cross the bridge and turn right to walk along the Fondementa.

Along the canal to the left you can see the Palazzo Cicogna, with its attractive Gothic windows. It is now used as a school.

The canal turns sharply left. Continue and pass one bridge. When you reach the next two bridges take the one to the right and bear left alongside the canal. Before the next two bridges turn right. Take the second bridge and turn right onto Fondementa Minotto, leading into Calle Vinanti. As you cross the canal take the next left over the bridge with the Scuola Grande di San Rocco (▶ 48–49) in front of you. Turn right, keeping the scuola to the left. Ahead is the church of Santa Maria Gloriosa dei Frari (▶ 44–45) with its superb interior.

Distance 3.5km (2 miles)
Time 2 hours plus stops
Start point Ponte dell'Accademia ✚ 138 D4
End point Santa Maria Gloriosa dei Frari ✚ 138 A3
Lunch Campo Santa Margherita (▶ 95) is a lively square with a choice of restaurants and cafés

PALAZZO DARIO

This must have the most picturesque façade of any Venetian palace, made even more interesting by the fact it leans alarmingly. It was built in the 1480s and was probably the work of architect Pietro Lombardo. The use of the beautiful inlaid coloured marbles is also seen in his masterpiece, Santa Maria dei Miracoli (➤ 83). There has been a long-standing legend that the Palazzo Dario is cursed. To get the best view look over from the Santa Maria del Giglio landing stage or when taking a trip on the Grand Canal.

✚ 139 D5 ✉ Calle Barbaro 🕔 Not open to the public 🚢 Giglio

PONTE DELL'ACCADEMIA

This is the widest crossing of the Grand Canal and surely the bridge with the loveliest of views. The canal's gentle curves, the boats and gondolas sail beneath you and the view of the dome of the Salute (➤ 46–47) is magical.

✚ 138 D4 ✉ Canal Grande 🚢 Accademia

IL REDENTORE

This is best seen across the water from the centre of Venice. Indeed, its architect, Palladio, who was commissioned to design it as an act of thanksgiving for the ending of a 16th-century plague, intended it to catch and hold the distant eye. The façade and the interior together form a magnificent example of what came to be known as Palladian architecture. On the third Sunday of July, a bridge of boats is constructed across the Giudecca Canal for the celebration of the Feast of the Redeemer (Redentore). The church is dramatically floodlit at night.

✚ 139 F7 (off map) ✉ Campo del Redentore, Giudecca Island 195 ☎ 041 523 1415 🕐 Mon–Sat 10–5, Sun 1–5; closed Sun in Jul and Aug 🖐 Inexpensive
🚢 Redentore

SANTA MARIA DEI CARMINI

Near the Campo Santa Margherita, this is a large and sombre 14th-century church, displaying many fine paintings, including a series in the nave illustrating the history of the Carmelite Order.

✚ 138 C2 ✉ Campo dei Carmini, Dorsoduro ☎ 041 522 6553 🕐 Mon–Sat 2:30–5:30 🖐 Free 🚢 San Basilio/Ca' Rezzonico

SANTA MARIA DELLA SALUTE

Best places to see, pages 46–47.

SAN NICOLÒ DEI MENDICOLI

This ornate yet modest parish church in a poor district of the city near the docks is one of Venice's oldest. Restored by British contributions to the Venice in Peril Fund in 1977, its gilded wooden statues gleam anew. Built between the 12th and 15th centuries and well-stocked with statuary and paintings, it is a good goal when exploring the hinterland of the western end of the Zattere and visiting the nearby churches of San Sebastiano and Angelo Raffaele.

✚ 138 C1 (off map) ✉ Campo San Nicolò, Dorsoduro 1907 ☎ 041 275 0382 🕐 Mon–Sat 10–12 ♿ Free 🚢 San Basilio/Ca' Rezzonico

SAN SEBASTIANO

The most important of the three major churches near the docks, it belongs to the great painter Paolo Veronese, who decorated it and is buried there. His works are everywhere in the church, including the open doors of the organ and the ceiling, in the chancel, the sacristy and the gallery, where he painted frescoes on the walls. In all, he painted here the richest and most comprehensive exhibition of his own

PAVLO CALIARIO
NATVRÆ ÆMVLO
SV ERST E FAT S

work and one that no admirer of Venetian art should miss. The interior of the church was restored during the 1980s and 1990s. It's worth using the audioguide.

✚ 138 D1 ⊠ Campo San Sebastiano, Dorsoduro 1686 ☎ 041 270 0462 ⏰ Mon–Sat 9–6, Sun 1–6 👋 Inexpensive 🚢 San Basilio/Ca' Rezzonico

SAN TROVASO

This is a huge Palladian church with two identical façades because, it is said, two rival 16th-century families each wanted to be the first to enter and so could do so simultaneously. The interior is lofty, light and peaceful; outside, the *campo* in front of the two main doors is a pleasant place to sit in the sun away from the city bustle.

✚ 138 D3 ⊠ Campo San Trovaso, Dorsoduro 1098 ☎ 041 522 2133 ⏰ Mon–Sat 3–6 👋 Free 🚢 Accademia/Zattere

SCUOLA GRANDE DEI CARMINI

This is the Venetian headquarters of the Carmelite order, founded in Palestine in 1235. Here the nuns undertake charitable work and attend services at the nearby church (➤ 103). Carmini had Giambattista Tiepolo (the elder) as its principal decorator in the 18th century and his flamboyant ceilings are the highlight of this *scuola*. His panels are in the Salone, on the upper floor, accessed via a stuccoed staircase. Although the themes are religious, his painting is sensual. They are not easy to understand but are based around the Carmelite emblem, the scapular, and are audacious works of art and a triumph of trompe l'oeil perspective.

✚ 138 C2 ⊠ Campo dei Carmini, Dorsoduro 2617 ☎ 041 528 9420 ⏰ Apr–Oct Mon–Sat 9–6, Sun 9–4; Nov–Mar daily 9–4 👋 Moderate 🚢 Ca' Rezzonico

SQUERO DI SAN TROVASO

This is a picturesque boatyard where gondolas have been built and repaired for hundreds of years, and it is still full of activity. Even though it is closed to the public you can get great photographs of the upturned gondolas awaiting repair, with the church of San Trovaso as a backdrop, all from the opposite side of the canal.

✚ 138 D3 ✉ On San Trovaso Canal (near the Zattere), Dorsoduro 🚤 Zattere

ZATTERE

The Zattere forms a series of *fondamente* (roads beside the water) along the Canal della Guidecca on the southern side of Dorsoduro. It stretches from the Stazione Márittima in the west to the Punta della Dogana in the east, its name deriving from the unloading of heavy goods – particulary cargos of salt for the nearby warehouses – which were floated to the quayside on rafts known as *záttere*. Ventians now love to take the *passeggiata* here and it is a great place to rest, have a drink or an ice cream.

✚ 138 E3 ✉ Zattere, Dorsoduro 🚤 Zattere/San Basilio

Lagoon Islands

Scattered across nearly 500sq km (200sq miles) of the Venetian lagoon are around 40 islands. Some have a proud history of their own; some were famous for their industries; others were renowned as religious centres.

Many of them acted as fortresses, gunpowder factories and stores; others were hospitals and asylums. Half of them are now deserted, while those still inhabited may be thriving communities or isolated institutions – a prison, a hospital or a religious retreat – and a few are used for public or private recreation. Some provide the fertile ground for vegetable crops to supply the Rialto's markets. Enough of them can be visited to add another dimension to a holiday in Venice. The main islands are well-serviced by vaporetto, but others can only be reached by the more expensive water taxis.

BURANO

The fishermen's and lacemakers' island with a population of about 5,000 lies more than 8km (5 miles) to the northeast of Venice. While Murano (► 110–111) is workaday and slightly dishevelled, Burano is neat and clean and its multi-coloured cottages lining little canals make it a perfect subject for photographs. Its character has been shaped by its industries – the robust way of life of its fishermen and boatbuilders and the delicacy of its lacemakers' skills. Usually women can be seen making lace outside the doors of their cottages – although they are now dwindling in number – and their products (as well as embroidery from Hong Kong) are on sale at stalls

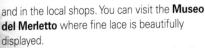

and in the local shops. You can visit the **Museo del Merletto** where fine lace is beautifully displayed.

There are few buildings of note, but the church of **San Martino** contains a huge and disturbing painting of the *Crucifixion* by the elder Tiepolo and has the most alarmingly tilted campanile of them all.

➕ 143 D5 🚤 LN from Fondamente Nuove

Museo del Merletto

✉ Piazza Galuppi 187 ☎ 041 730 034 🕐 Apr–Oct Wed–Mon 10–5; Nov–Mar Wed–Mon 10–4 ✋ Moderate

San Martino

✉ Piazza Galuppi ☎ 041 730 096 🕐 Daily 8–12, 3–7 ✋ Free

CHIOGGIA

Once an island, Chioggia is now, like Venice, connected to the mainland by a causeway; unlike Venice, several of its canals have been filled in to become roads for cars. In the far south of the lagoon, 26km (16 miles) from Venice, it has grown from a fishing port to an important town of some 55,000 inhabitants. Now, in essence, it belongs to the mainland rather than the lagoon.

Much of the town, particularly around the remaining canals, is reminiscent of Venice, and many buildings date from the 13th to 18th centuries. There are several fine churches, notably the Duomo, built between the 13th and 17th centuries, which contains a painting by the elder Tiepolo. There are a number of excellent fish restaurants near the harbour and in the Corso del Popolo.

➕ 142 E4 🚌 From Piazzale Roma 🚤 11 from the Lido

ℹ Museo Civico, Fondamenta San Francesco ☎ 041 550 0911

LIDO DI VENEZIA

This is the only one of the Venetian islands to have roads, and its buses, cars and lorries are imported by ferry from the mainland. A little to the southeast of Venice, it is just over 11km (7 miles) long and 1km (half a mile) wide, covering the largest sand bank between the lagoon and the Adriatic. With a population of about 20,000 it is essentially a seaside holiday resort and is crowded in summer, when it is also host to the International Film Festival.

It was at its most fashionable before World War I as the architecture of its hotels and villas testifies, and its long sandy beach is still lined with the old wooden bathing-huts. Look for some interesting art nouveau and art deco buildings. Of particular interest on the Gran Viale is the Hungaria Palace and No 14, the Villa Monplaisir. Another striking building is the Grand Hotel Excelsior Palace, sporting its very own minaret. There's also the historic church of San Nicolò, founded in 1044, at the northern end of the island. The doge came here on Ascension Day after the ceremony of marrying Venice to the sea.

From the *vaporetto* bound from the Lido to San Marco, Venice is seen as it was intended it should first be seen, from the deck of a ship approaching from the sea, its towers, domes and palaces materializing between water and sky in one of the great spectacles of the world.

➕ 143 E5 🚌 ACTV buses leave for all destinations on the Lido 🚢 1 from San Zaccaria or stops on the Grand Canal

ℹ️ Viale Santa Maria Elisabetta 6/a, Lido di Venezia ☎ 041 526 5721

🕐 Jun–Sep daily 8:30–7:30

MURANO

With around 5,000 inhabitants, Murano lies a short distance to the north of the city. It is an industrial island and has the feel of a small working town, although some of its factories lie derelict. Glass is its product and has been since the 13th century, when production was moved out of Venice itself because of the fire risk. Venetian glass has long been a curious mixture of the beautiful and the vulgar, whether in table-glass, ornaments, mirrors or chandeliers. Past products can be see in the **Museo del Vetro,** together with a history of glass on the island. New production can be seen in many factory showrooms.

Murano is a miniature, shabbier Venice with its own scaled-down Canal Grande, crossed by a single bridge. Its most notable building is the church of **Santa Maria e Donato,** which has a 12th-century mosaic floor and a 15th-century 'ship's keel' roof.

➕ 142 E4 🚤 41 or DM

Museo del Vetro

✉ Fondamenta Giustinian 8, Isola di Murano ☎ 041 739 586 🕐 Apr–Oct Thu–Tue 10–5; Nov–Mar Thu–Tue 10–4 🖐 Moderate 🚤 To Museo

Santa Maria e Donato

✉ Campo San Donato ☎ 041 739 056 🕐 Mon–Sat 9–12, 3:30–7, Sun 3:30–7 🖐 Free 🚤 To Museo

SAN FRANCESCO DEL DESERTO

This remote and peaceful island can be reached by ferry from Burano, and the resident friars will show visitors the 13th-century cloister and the church of the hermitage, where St Francis of Assisi is said to have stayed.

www.isola-sanfrancescodeldeserto.it

✚ 143 E5 ☎ 041 528 6863 🕓 Irregular hours; phone or see website for details ✋ Donation on admission 🛥 Water taxi from ✉ Burano

SAN LAZZARO DEGLI ARMENI

This Armenian island can be visited to see the church, library and monastery where Lord Byron stayed in 1817 to learn Armenian.

✚ 142 E4 ☎ 041 526 0104 🕓 Daily guided tour 3:25–4:25 ✋ Moderate 🛥 20

SAN MICHELE

This is the cemetery island, as can be seen by its sepulchral white walls and the tall, dark cypress trees beyond. The beautiful 15th-century church of San Michele in Isola is of interest to students of Renaissance artchitecture, but the cemetery is even sadder than could be expected, for dead Venetians cannot rest there long. While the famous – such as the composer Stravinsky, the poet Ezra Pound and the ballet impresario Diaghilev – are allowed to remain, nearly all Venetians buried here are disinterred after a period and their bones scattered on a reef made of their ancestors' remains in a remote reach of the lagoon. Visitors cannot fail to appreciate that here death, as well as life, is transitory.

✚ 137 B7 🚢 41, 42 to Cimitero (cemetry)

TORCELLO

If you only visit one island make it Torcello. It was the first island to be settled by refugees from the barbarian invasion of the 5th century. At the height of its power, the population was said to have numbered 20,000, but the growth of the more distant and secure Venice, the silting of its creek and the prevalence of malaria reduced it to the level of the other small islands of the lagoon by the 15th century. Now the permanent popluation is only around 20 people, increased slighty in the summer by restaurant staff.

Lying close to the mainland marshes and more than 10 km (6 miles) to the northeast of Venice, the little green island offers peace after the bustling city and relaxation in walks along its narrow footpaths. Its great monument is the cathedral of **Santa Maria dell'Assunta,** where the extraordinary Byzantine mosaics – notably a tall and compelling Madonna and Child and a vast depiction of Judgement Day – have been restored. The basilica dates from 638 and is the oldest building in Venice. It remains virtually untouched since alterations in the 11th century.

The whole island, including the cathedral, the small church of Santa Fosco, the archaeological museum, **Museo dell'Estuario** and the surrounding farmland, is easily explored and can be combined with lunch on a day-trip from Venice without making an early start or expecting a late return.

✚ 143 D5 🚢 LN from Fondamente Nuove, 'T' from Burano

Basilica di Santa Maria dell'Assunta

✉ Torcello ☎ 041 296 0630, 041 521 2362 🕒 Mar–Oct daily 10:30–6; Nov–Feb daily 10–5 ✋ Moderate

Museo dell'Estuario

✉ Torcello ☎ 041 270 2464 🕒 Mar–Oct Tue–Sun 10:30–6; Nov–Feb Tue–Sun 10–5 ✋ Moderate

around the Isole Venezia

In the Lagoon north of Venice is an archipelago of flat little islands. Many of these are uninhabited or privately owned, but some have been populated for centuries. Three – Murano, Burano and Torcello – each in a different way, are interesting places to visit on a day trip from Venice.

From San Zaccaria the boat heads southeast past the island of San Giorgio Maggiore.

The church here (1559–80), by Palladio, contains works by Tintoretto and has excellent views from its bell tower.

The boat then chugs round the eastern peninsula of Venice before heading northwest, past the Isola di San Michele.

The island has been used as a graveyard since the 19th century; Diaghilev, Stravinsky and Ezra Pound are among those who lie behind its protective walls.

North of here is the island of Murano.

The centre of Venetian glass-blowing since the 13th century, Murano has numerous factories offering guided tours and the Museo del Vetro with glass pieces from the 15th century onward. This island is like a miniature Venice with its own Grand Canal.

Next comes Burano.

Once a great lace-making hub, Burano is now more remarkable for its brightly painted houses – purple, sky blue, leaf green and more – and the alarmingly leaning tower of San Martino church. Walk in the back streets to avoid the crowds and you will see that time has stood still, the washing still hangs out and the locals tend their pretty balconies and pots of bright flowers.

Torcello, the last, is the most historic, reached by the 'T' shuttle boat from Burano.

Torcello was once a thriving community of 20,000, but started to decline in the 14th century. Now all that remain are two adjoining churches set in serene rural scenery near an old canal. The 9th- to 11th-century Cathedral of Santa Maria dell'Assunta has a charmingly expressive mosaic of the Last Judgement, while the 12th-century church of Santa Fosca is surrounded on three sides by a harmonious peristyle (row of columns) and has a tranquil, simple interior.

Distance 20km (12 miles)
Time Allow about 2.5–3 hours without stops; up to a day with stops
Start/end point San Zaccaria *vaparetto* stop ✚ 141 C5
Lunch Locanda Cipriani ✉ Torcelllo 29 ☎ 041 730 150

Excursions

ASOLO

The most beautiful of the hinterland towns, Asolo lies in
the foothills of the Alps 64km (40 miles) from Venice. A
charming town of some 6,000 inhabitants, its old houses
– sometimes arcaded at street level as is the custom in
hill towns – cluster around squares and narrow streets
and overlook a landscape decorated with villas and
cypress trees.

✚ 142 C3 🚌 No direct bus to Asolo. It is possible to get a train to
Bassano del Grappa, then bus towards Montebelluna and a shuttle
to Asolo. Car or tour easiest

🛈 Piazza Garibaldi 73 ☎ 0423 529 046

BASSANO DEL GRAPPA

In the foothills of the Alps, nearly 80km (50 miles) northwest of Venice, this town of 37,000 inhabitants was once
under Venetian rule. Formerly renowned for its school of
painting, it now produces colourful pottery, which is sold
in Venice and throughout northern Italy.

There are some fine old buildings and a famous
covered wooden bridge – the Ponte degli Coperto –
that has been rebuilt several times since the early 13th
century. Bassano is noted for the strong alcoholic spirit,
grappa. The town is a good base for exploring the
mountains – particularly Monte Grappa, which was an
Italian stronghold during World War I – and the battlefields
Ernest Hemingway described in *A Farewell to Arms*.

Farther north and into the Alps is the handsome old
town of Belluno and beyond it the Dolomite mountains
and the celebrated resort of Cortina, renowned for winter
sports and summer walking. Austria is also just within
range of a day's excursion.

✚ 142 C3 🚉 From Venezia San Lucia station

🛈 Largo Corona d'Italia 35 ☎ 0424 524 351

BELLUNO

This attractive town, the
capital of Belluno province and
90km (56 miles) from Venice,
is at the junction of the flat
plains of Veneto to the south
and the stunning Dolomite
mountains to the north. It
claimed the accolade of 'Alpine
Town of the Year in 1999' but it
is often overlooked by people
in their rush to see the
mountains. There is much
more to Belluno than being
the starting point for a hiking
or a skiing holiday. Its
architecture reflects its close
proximity to Venice and
merges well with the rural
style of the surrounding
countryside. Highlights of the
town include the spectacular
views from the 12th-century
Porta Rugo and from the bell
tower of the 16th-century
Duomo. Take a break in the
town's finest square, Piazza
del Mercato, complete with
fountain and arcaded
Renaissance palaces.

➕ 142 B4 🚆 From Venezia San
Lucia station
ℹ️ Piazza dei Martiri 7
☎ 0437 940 083

DOLOMITI

The Dolomite mountains look as if they've been carved, folded and squeezed into an extraordinary variety of gnarled crags. They are named after Frenchman Déodat Tancrè Gratet de Domomieu (1750–1801), who was responsible for discovering the chemical component that renders the local rock so different from others. Although this is Italy, the language, scenery, architecture and much of the culture have been strongly influenced by Austria, and in particular in the north of the region, on the far side of the Dolomites, nearly all the place names have versions in German.

It is possible to take tours from Venice to the mountains, where you will witness soaring peaks, deep verdant valleys, emerald lakes and enchanting mountain villages. Some tours take you as far as Cortina d'Ampezzo, one of Italy's top ski and alpine resorts. There are plenty of superb photo opportunities. Activities in the mountains include rambling along the footpaths and picnicking, mountain biking, skiing in season and the use of chairlifts to get to see some of the most breathtaking scenery. The range of flora is extensive: look for the gorgeous orange mountain lily, pretty saxigfrages, the purple gentian (among a dozen gentian species) – its roots are used to make a local liqueur – the black vanilla, globe and lady's slipper orchids, and the enigmatic devil's claw. Butterflies abound, and you may see eagles, chamois and the Alpine marmot, too.

The closest Dolomite town to Venice, lying in the foothills of the mountains, is Belluno (▶ 121). This is a far cry from the German-speaking northern Dolomites, but there is an Alpine air pervading. Close by is the Parco Naturale delle Dolomiti Bellunesi, an environmental project protecting the countryside and cultural heritage of the area. Tourists have been visiting since the 18th century, drawn by the spectacular scenery and Alpine plants and flowers. The park is actively promoting the continuation of the traditional environment by encouraging old farming methods and thus leaving the locality virtually unchanged. This is a fascinating region and a total contrast from the low-lying area of Venice and its islands.

🚹 142 A3 🚆 To Belluno from Venezia San Lucia station ❓ By arranged tour, car or bus. Information from Venice tourist office or local travel agencies

LIDO DI JÉSOLO

This seaside resort is along the Adriatic coast 40km (25 miles) to the east of Venice and can be reached by bus from the city. Its sandy beach is 15km (9 miles) long and offers accommodation from hotels to villas and apartments to campsites. Although there has been a settlement here since Roman times it only developed as a thriving resort after World War I and now more than 400,000 people visit every year. You can participate in all manner of activities: sailing, horse riding, go karting and, of course, swimming as well as enjoying a vibrant nightlife.
www.jesolo.it

➕ 143 D5 🚤 The easiest way to get to Jésolo is by bus and then by boat. Ask at the tourist office

ℹ Piazza Brescia 13 ☎ 0421 370 601/602/603; also in summer at Piazza Torino ☎ 0421 363 607

PADOVA (PADUA)

The nearest large town to Venice, with a population of 250,000,
Padova can be reached by train, bus, car – or by boat. For the latter,
the *Burchiello* and its rival the *Ville del Brenta*, sail between April
and October from San Marco at about 9am (times and fares
available from hotels, travel agents and tourist information offices),
cross the lagoon and cruise up the Brenta Canal, which is, in fact,
a river. Stopping at several magnificent Renaissance villas on its
banks and for lunch at a riverside restaurant, the boats arrive at
Padua between 6 and 6.30pm and the 37km (23-mile) return
journey to Venice is made by bus or train. A Venetian university
city since the 15th century – and rich in buildings of that century –
Padova is now dominated by commerce.

www.turismopadova.it

142 E3 53E From Venezia San Lucia station

Galleria Pedrocchi ☎ 049 876 7927; Piazzale del
Stazione ☎ 049 875 2077; Mar–Apr also Piazza del
Santo ☎ 049 875 3087

POSSAGNO

Anyone eager to see more works of art should visit the village of Possagno, 72km (45 miles) northwest of Venice, the home of the sculptor Antonio Canova. Born here in 1757, Canova became the greatest of the neoclassical sculptors, producing smoothly graceful figures and delicate portraits, including his famous busts of Napoleon and Josephine.

His house is now the centre of a gallery devoted to his works, mostly plaster models for statuary, and in the parish church which he gave to the village – the Tempio di Canova, inspired by the Parthenon in Athens and the Pantheon in Rome – is his tomb. However, only his body lies here; his heart remains in Venice, within the pyramid he himself designed for Titian in the great church of the Frari (➤ 44–45).

✚ 142 C3 ⊠ From Venezia San Lucia station to Bassano del Grappa then bus to Possagno (1 hour)

TREVISO

Treviso's walled centre is full of meandering old streets and brooding canals. The medieval and Renaissance buildings of Piazza dei Signori include the church of Santa Lucia, with frescoes by Tommaso da Modena (14th century). Gothic San Nicolò contains more da Modena frescoes on the columns as well as works by Lorenzo Lotto and others, while the 15th- to 16th-century

cathedral has a Titian altarpiece and an
11th-century baptistery. There is good
Renaissance art in the Museo Civico.
www.provincia.turismo.it
🔼 142 D4 🚌 8E 🚆 From Venezia San Lucia station
🛈 Piazzetta Monte di Pietà 8 ☎ 0422 547 632

TRIESTE
Farther east of Venice than Lido di Jésolo is
the great seaport of Trieste, once part of the
Austro-Hungarian Empire and connected to
Venice by rail. A little farther the north, just
across the Slovenian border, is Lipica, where
the Lipizzaner white horses are bred.
www.triestetourism.it
🔼 143 D8 🚌 3, 6, 57, 66 🚆 From Venezia San
Lucia station
🛈 Piazza Unità d'Italia 4B ☎ 040 347 8312

VERONA

Verona lies west of Vicenza (➤ opposite), close to Lake Garda and
some 98km (61 miles) from Venice. It is the second-biggest city
in the Veneto region after Venice. It is most famous as the setting
of Shakespeare's play *Romeo and Juliet* and for its Roman
remains, notably a magnificent arena, which is sometimes used
for performances of opera. Among Verona's other important
monuments is the unusually ornate Romanesque church of San
Zeno Maggiore (1123–35), with 11th–12th century bronze door
panels, a 'ship's keel' ceiling (1376) and an altarpiece by Mantegna
(1450s). The two main squares are the elegant Piazza dei Signori,
with the 12th-century Palazzo del Comune (town hall) among its
medieval and Renaissance civic gems, and the more workaday

Piazza delle Erbe, with a busy market. The powerful Scaligeri family, who governed the town from 1260 to 1387, are commemorated by a 14th-century bridge leading to the Castelvecchio (with an excellent art collection) and by the Arche Scaligere, their opulent tombs.

www.tourism.verona.it

✚ 142 D1 🚊 From Venezia San Lucia station

🛈 Piazza Bra, Via degli Alpini 9 ☎ 045 806 8680

VICENZA

The capital of the Veneto is Vicenza, which lies 51km (32 miles) from Venice and is a handsome city, where the great architect Andrea di Palladio – a native of Padova – designed a dozen buildings.

Most famous of these is his eye-pleasingly symmetrical villa La Rotunda, which has been copied all over the world. Palladio's first public commission was the graceful double-colonnaded Basilica in Piazza dei Signori, where he also designed the Loggia del Capitaniato. Among the mass of other Palladio buildings are the Teatro Olimpico (1579), the oldest covered theatre in Europe, and many of the palazzi on Corso Andrea Palladio. The Museo Civico (in another Palladio building) has splendid Gothic and Renaissance art. Other older monuments include the Gothic churches of Santa Corona and San Lorenzo and some buildings on Contrà Porti, untouched by Palladio.

www.vicenza.org

✚ 142 D2 🚊 From Venezia San Lucia station

🛈 Piazza Matteotti 12 ☎ 0444 320 854; also office at Piazza dei Signori 8
☎ 0444 544 122

Index

Acknowledgements

The Automobile Association would like to thank the following photographers, companies and picture libraries for their assistance in the preparation of this book.

Abbreviations for the picture credits are as follows – (t) top; (b) bottom; (c) centre; (l) left; (r) right; (AA) AA World Travel Library.

4l Carnival, AA/D Miterdiri; **4c** Santa Maria della Salute, AA/A Mockford & N Bonetti; **4r** Fondamenta Zattere, AA/S McBride; **5l** Cortina d'Ampezzo, Belluno, Fototeca ENIT; **5c** Santa Maria della Salute, AA/C Sawyer; **5r** Grand Canal, AA/A Mockford & N Bonetti; **6** Bridge of Sighs, AA/A Mockford & N Bonetti; **7** Santa Maria della Salute interior, AA/A Mockford & N Bonetti; **8** Ca' d'Oro, AA/A Mockford & N Bonetti; **9** Palazzo Ducale, AA/A Mockford & N Bonetti; **10** Mask shop, AA/A Mockford & N Bonetti; **11** Gondola, AA/A Mockford & N Bonetti; **12** Flags of San Marco, AA/A Mockford & N Bonetti; **13** Restaurant, AA/A Mockford & N Bonetti; **14/15** Carnival, AA/D Miterdiri; **18** Carnival, AA/D Miterdiri; **20** Marco Polo airport, AA/C Sawyer; **21tr** Vaporetto, AA/A Mockford & N Bonetti; **21cl** Gondola, AA/S McBride; **22** Water taxi, AA/S McBride; **25** Pharmacy sign, AA/A Mockford & N Bonetti; **26** Carabinieri, AA/A Mockford & N Bonetti; **28/29** Santa Maria della Salute, AA/A Mockford & N Bonetti; **30/31** Piazza San Marco, AA/A Mockford & N Bonetti; **31** Cupola, AA/C Sawyer; **32/33b** Palazzo on the Grand Canal, AA/C Sawyer; **32/33t** Palazzo Dario, AA/C Sawyer; **34/35t** Bellini and Giorgione canvases, AA/A Mockford & N Bonetti; **34/35b** Vivarini paintings, AA/A Mockford & N Bonetti; **36** Palazzo Ducale, AA/A Mockford & N Bonetti; **36/37** Gothic tracery, AA/A Mockford & N Bonetti; **38/39** Piazza San Marco, AA/A Mockford & N Bonetti; **39** Feeding pigeons, AA/A Mockford & N Bonetti; **40/41** San Giorgio Maggiore, AA/S McBride; **42/43b** Santi Giovanni e Paolo interior, AA/S McBride; **42/43t** Exterior, AA/S McBride; **43** Tomb of Doge Michele Steno, AA/R Newton; **44bl** Monument to Antonio Canova, AA/C Sawyer; **44cr** Statue, AA/S McBride; **44/45** Choir stalls, AA/C Sawyer; **46** Entrance detail, AA/S McBride; **46/47** Grand Canal and Santa Maria della Salute, AA/S McBride; **48** San Rocco exterior, AA/A Mockford & N Bonetti; **48/49** Interior, AA/A Mockford & N Bonetti; **49** Sign, AA/A Mockford & N Bonetti; **50/51** Fondamenta Zattere, AA/S McBride; **52** Basilica di San Marco, AA/S McBride; **54** Caffè Florian, AA/A Mockford & N Bonetti; **54/55** Campanile di San Marco, AA/A Mockford & N Bonetti; **56** Portrait of Doge Giovanni Mocenigo by Gentile Bellini, AA/D Miterdiri; **57** Palazzo Contarini del Bovolo, AA/A Mockford & N Bonetti; **58/59** The Education of the Virgin by Tiepolo, AA/A Mockford & N Bonetti; **59** San Moisè, AA/S McBride; **60** Street signs, AA/C Sawyer; **61** La Fenice sign, AA/C Sawyer; **62/63** San Salvador, AA/A Mockford & N Bonetti; **64** Torre dell'Orologio, AA/R Newton; **65** San Francesco della Vigna, AA/D Miterdiri; **66/67** Canal near Campo Santa Maria Formosa, AA/A Mockford & N Bonetti; **68** Ceremonial barge, AA/C Sawyer; **68/69** Riva degli Schiavoni, AA/S McBride; **70** Giardini Pubblici, AA/S McBride; **70/71** Castello district, AA/S McBride; **72/73** San Giovanni in Bragora, AA/A Mockford & N Bonetti; **72** San Giorgio dei Greci, AA/D Miterdiri; **73** Santa Maria Formosa, AA/A Mockford & N Bonetti; **74/75** Scuola Grande di San Marco, AA/S McBride; **75** Statue, San Zaccaria, AA/D Miterdiri; **76** Scuola di San Giorgio degli Schiavoni, AA/D Miterdiri; **77** Ca' d'Oro lion statues, AA/A Mockford & N Bonetti; **78** Ca' d'Oro loggia shadows, AA/A Mockford & N Bonetti; **78/79** Campo dei Mori, AA/A Mockford & N Bonetti; **80** Madonna dell'Orto, AA/S McBride; **80/81** Sant'Alvise interior, AA/A Mockford & N Bonetti; **82** San Geremia e Lucia, AA/A Mockford & N Bonetti; **82/83** Santa Maria dei Miracoli, AA/A Mockford & N Bonetti; **84** Santa Maria di Nazaretha, AA/A Mockford & N Bonetti; **85** San Stae, AA/A Mockford & N Bonetti; **86/87** Campo San Polo, AA/A Mockford & N Bonetti; **87** Rialto fish market, AA/A Mockford & N Bonetti; **88/89** On the Rialto Bridge, AA/A Mockford & N Bonetti; **90/91** San Pantalon, AA/S McBride; **92** Gondolier, AA/A Mockford & N Bonetti; **93** Campo San Barnaba, AA/S McBride; **94** Ca' Rezzonico, AA/C Sawyer; **94/95** Campo San Barnaba, AA/S McBride; **96tr** Gardens of the Peggy Guggenheim Collection, AA/S McBride; **96cr** Dogana di Mare, AA/D Miterdiri; **97** Peggy Guggenheim Collection, AA/S McBride; **98/99** La Giudecca island, AA/S McBride; **98** Gesuati, AA/C Sawyer; **100** Campo Santa Margherita, AA/A Mockford & N Bonetti; **100/101** Pulpit detail in Angelo Raffaele, AA/A Mockford & N Bonetti; **102/103b** Accademia bridge, AA/A Mockford & N Bonetti; **102/103t** Il Redentore, AA/A Mockford & N Bonetti; **103** Santa Maria dei Carmini interior, AA/A Mockford & N Bonetti; **104/105** Statue of Veronese, San Sebastiano, AA/A Mockford & N Bonetti; **106tl** Squero di San Trovaso, AA/D Miterdiri; **106b** Zattere, AA/S McBride; **107** Hungaria Palace Hotel, the Lido, AA/A Mockford & N Bonetti; **108/109t** Burano, AA/C Sawyer; **108/109b** Lacemaking, AA/S McBride; **110/111** Murano glass beads, AA/A Mockford & N Bonetti; **112/113** San Michele, AA/A Mockford & N Bonetti; **114/115** Basilica Santa Maria dell'Assunta, Torcello, AA/A Mockford & N Bonetti; **116** Murano glass, AA/C Sawyer; **116/117** Lagoon, AA/D Miterdiri; **118/119** Cortina d'Ampezzo, Belluno, Fototeca ENIT; **120/121** Belluno, Fototeca ENIT; **122** Monte Cristallo, Belluno, Fototeca ENIT; **122/123** Cortina d'Ampezzo, Belluno, Fototeca ENIT; **124/125** Prato della Valle, Padova, Fototeca ENIT; **126/127** Grounds of the Duomo, Treviso, AA/C Sawyer; **127** Piazza dell'Unita d'Italia, Trieste, Fototeca ENIT; **128/129** Teatro Romano, Verona, AA/A Mockford & N Bonetti; **129** Roman gate, Verona, AA/A Mockford & N Bonetti.

Every effort has been made to trace the copyright holders, and we apologise in advance for any accidental errors. We would be happy to apply the corrections in the following edition of this publication.

Maps

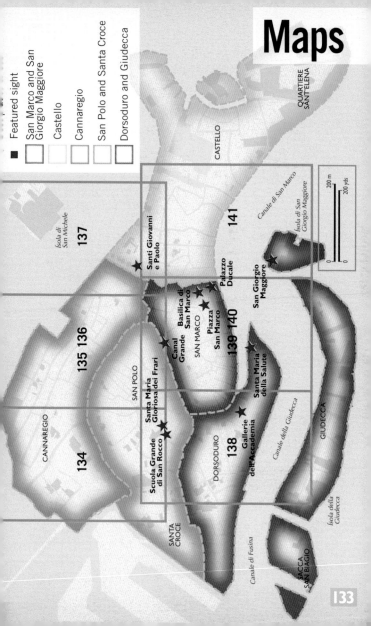

Featured sight

- San Marco and San Giorgio Maggiore
- Castello
- Cannaregio
- San Polo and Santa Croce
- Dorsoduro and Giudecca

Isola di San Michele

137

135 136

134

CANNAREGIO

SANTA CROCE

SAN POLO

DORSODURO

138

Scuola Grande di San Rocco

Santa Maria Gloriosa dei Frari

Gallerie dell'Accademia

Santa Maria della Salute

Canal Grande

SAN MARCO

Basilica di San Marco

Piazza San Marco

139 140

Palazzo Ducale

Santi Giovanni e Paolo

San Giorgio Maggiore

CASTELLO

141

QUARTIERE SANT'ELENA

Canale di San Marco

Isola di San Giorgio Maggiore

GIUDECCA

Canale della Giudecca

Isola della Giudecca

Canale di Fusina

SACCA SAN BIAGIO

0   200 m
0   200 yds

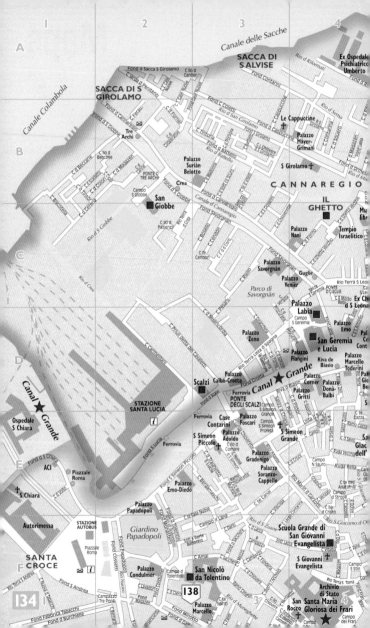

Map coordinates (top): **5** · **6** · **7** · **8**
Map rows (right): **A** · **B** · **C** · **D** · **E**

Sant Alvise

Canale delle Navi

Ospedale
Fatebenefratelli

Madonna dell'Orto

Sant'Alvise
Convento

Casino
d Spiriti

Scuola
di Mercanti

Madonna
dell'Orto

**QUARTIERE
GRIMANI**

Palazzo
Minelli

Palazzo
Mastelli

Palazzo
Contarini
d Zaffo

**Campo
dei Mori**

Palazzo
Longo

Casa
Tintoretto

Sacca della
Misericordia

Scuola Vecchia
d Misericordia

Ex Convento
S M d Servi

Cappella d
Volta Santo

S Marziale

S Maria
Valverde

Scuola Nuova
di Misericordia

Ex Chiesa
di S Caterina

137

Palazzo
Diedo

Palazzo
Lezze

Palazzo
Molin

Palazzo
Papafava

Oratorio d
Oratolio d
dei Crociferi

La Maddalena

Palazzo Corrèr
Contarini

S Fosca

Palazzo
Vendramin

Palazzo
Zen

Ex Convento

San
Marcuola

Campo
S Marcuola

Palazzo Vendramin-
Calergi (Casinò)

San Marcuola

S Felice

Palazzo
Seriman

Canal
Fondaco
dei Turchi

Palazzo
Belloni
Battaglia

Ca'
Tron

Grande

Palazzo
Molin
Barbarigo

Palazzo Barbaro

Palazzo
Emo

Palazzo
Giovanelli

Museo
di Storia
Naturale

Palazzo
Priuli-
Bon

San Stae

Palazzo Gussoni-
Grimani della Vida

Palazzo
Fontana

Palazzo
Boldù

Ca'
d'Oro

S Sofia

Palazzo
Priuli-Stazio

San Stae

Palazzo
Foscarini-
Giovanelli

Museo del
Tessuto e
del Costume

Ca' Pesaro

Palazzo Donà

Palazzo Corner
della Regina

Casa
Favretto

Ca' d'Oro

Palazzo
Foscari

Santi
Apostoli

**Palazzo
Mocenigo**

S Maria
Mater Domini

Palazzo
Agnus Dio

Palazzo
Brandolin

Palazzo
Sagredo

Palazzo
Michiel
dalle Colonne

Scuola
d'Angelo
Custode

S Sofia

San
Canz

Palazzo
Grioni

Palazzo
Zane

San
Cassiano

S San
Giovanni
Decollato

Campo
Nuova

Pescheria
Campo de Pescaria

Ca' da
Mosto

San Giovanni
Crisostomo

Palazzo
Gozzi

Palazzo
Moro

Campo
Muti-Baglioni

Fabbriche
Nuove

Lion-Morosini

Teatro
Malibran

Palazzo
Grioni

Palazzo
Molin-Cappella

San Giovanni
Elemosinario

Fabbriche
Vecchie

Mercato
di Rialto

Palazzo
Bembo e Boldù

Palazzo
Bernardo

Palazzo
Albrizzi

S Aponal

Gobbo
di Rialto

S Giacomo
di Rialto

Erberia

Fondaco
dei Tedeschi

Palazzo
Bragadin
Carabba

Palazzo
Corner
Mocenigo

SAN POLO

**Campo
San Polo**

Palazzo
Soranzo

139

San Polo

Palazzo
Maffetti-
Tiepolo

S Silvestro

S Aponal

Campo
Rialto
Nuovo

Dieci Savi

**PONTE
DI RIALTO**

Rialto

San Bartolomeo

Grande

135

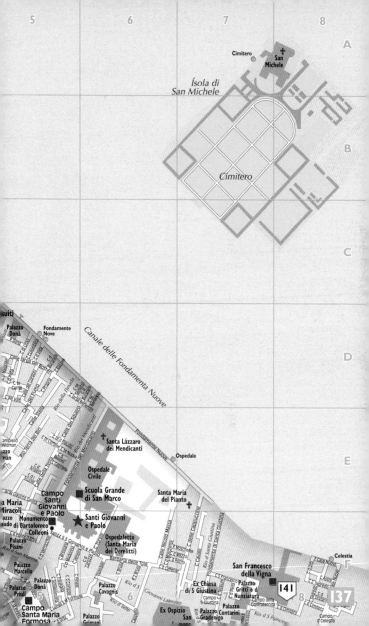

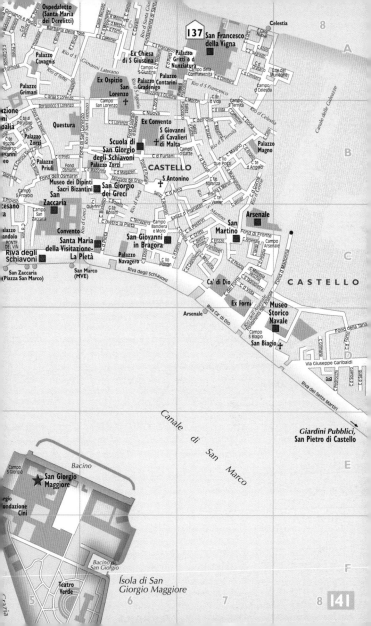

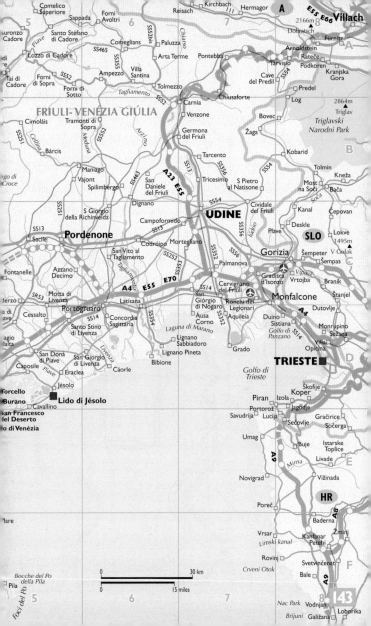

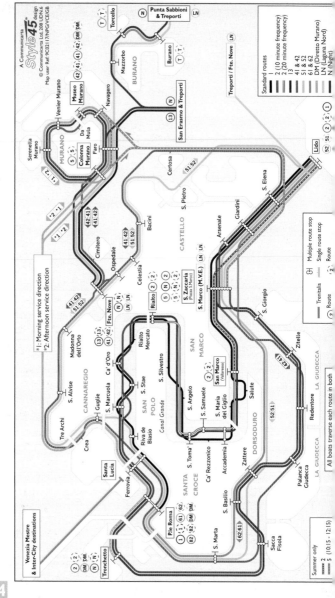

144